NOTHING ELSE TO FEAR

"In *Nothing Else To Fear* David Ellis skilfully weaves together strands of his gripping personal encounters with fear with the strong threads of biblical teaching. Here is the experience of a seasoned and respected missionary, pastor, family man and Christian strategist expressed with a vibrant and contagious enthusiasm for Christ and the gospel. Here is the robust kind of biblical wisdom we all need." – *Rev. Dr Sinclair Ferguson, Westminster Theological Seminary, Dallas, Texas*

"Ellis draws on his own exciting experiences and on contemporary events, but bases his work firmly on the Scriptures. And he writes in a way that even a new believer will understand and be nourished and challenged by. Thrown in as a bonus is a sensitive and helpful description of the Islamic world and how Christians should respond to it. I need to read books like this regularly to help maintain my spiritual glow." – *Ajith Fernando, Youth for Christ, Sri Lanka*

"The absolute trustworthiness of God and his Word, even in the face of tragedy or turmoil, is the deep-down bedrock of this book. David Ellis writes with passion and compassion, weaving together Scripture and personal experience. He does not dodge the reality of awesome suffering, but affirms the triumph of God over evil, a triumph with a crucified Saviour at its heart. A tender, pastoral, faith-building read." – *Rose Dowsett, Chairman, Interserve International and author of* Thinking Clearly about the Great Commission

PUBLISHING

OMF International works in most East Asian countries, and among East Asian peoples around the world. It was founded by James Hudson Taylor in 1865 as the China Inland Mission. Our purpose is to glorify God through the urgent evangelisation of East Asia's billions.

In line with this, OMF Publishing seeks to motivate and equip Christians to make disciples of all peoples. Publications include:

- stories and biographies showing God at work in East Asia
- the biblical basis of mission and mission issues
- the growth and development of the Church in Asia
- studies of Asian culture and religion

Books, booklets, articles and free downloads can be found on our website at *www.omf.org*

Addresses for OMF English-speaking centres can be found at the back of this book.

Nothing Else To Fear

Holding fast to God in tough times

DAVID W. ELLIS

MONARCH
BOOKS
Mill Hill, London & Grand Rapids, Michigan

Overseas Missionary Fellowship

First published by Monarch Books in the UK in 2003,
Concorde House, Grenville Place,
Mill Hill, London, NW7 3SA.

Published in the USA by Monarch Books 2004.

Distributed by:
UK: STL, PO Box 300, Kingstown Broadway, Carlisle,
Cumbria CA3 0QS;
USA: Kregel Publications, PO Box 2607,
Grand Rapids, Michigan 49501.

ISBN 1 85424 637 2 (UK)
ISBN 0 8254 6235 5 (USA)

British Library Cataloguing Data
A catalogue record for this book is available
from the British Library.

Book design and production for the publishers by
Bookprint Creative Services
P.O. Box 827, BN21 3YJ, England.
Printed in Great Britain.

CONTENTS

FOREWORD

I have cherished the friendship of David and Adèle Ellis for more years than we would care to admit. We first met when I made a brief foray into the old Glasgow Bible Training Institute in Bothwell Street. David and Adèle were both BTI students at the time.

The first thing I heard about David Ellis was that he was one of the truly outstanding students in the college. The second thing I heard was that he was pursuing the Principal's daughter, Adèle: successfully, as we were all delighted to hear, for it was very obviously God who had brought them together. They were an example to all their contemporaries in wisdom, grace and spiritual maturity.

Before long, they were called to Indonesia, to serve with the Overseas Missionary Fellowship. Within a fairly short period, David clearly emerged as a leader in the Indonesian field, even amongst the outstanding people serving God there with OMF.

When in the early 1970s I visited Indonesia, on behalf of OMF, he was Field Superintendant. During these memorable weeks, we travelled throughout most of Java to field and pastors' conferences. David acted as my remarkably fluent translator, and highly skilful driver. His ability with languages was extraordinary: the pastors often told me that he spoke like a native, even using accents and dialects which were appropriate to the region wherever we were. One of them came uncomfortably close to the truth when he smilingly described our combined attempts at preaching and interpreting in these words, "Pak Ellis make very good sermons for you."

I was deeply impressed by David's vision for these men. So many people in Indonesia had professed faith in Christ, and he saw that their great need was to be brought under a biblical and expository ministry. So he sought to teach the pastors how to expound God's word. By example and instruction he became a true "pastor of pastors" to them.

I have often wished that some biographical account of the Ellises' years in Indonesia might be written, and that some of David's expositions I had heard in various places might be available for the profit of the wider Christian church. In *Nothing Else to Fear* both wishes are fulfilled. This book is a record, from days of violent revolution and constant danger, of how two servants of God stood steadfast, with their confidence in the sovereign Lord. No wonder Psalm 2 came to mean so much to them. The exposition of that Psalm, and of other parts of Scripture, is woven through the extraordinary narrative of events through which they lived. It would have been almost impossible for David to do the one without the other.

Of course those of us who worshipped in St George's-Tron Church in Glasgow in the 1980s will recognise the God-centred biblical ministry with which David enriched our lives when he and I were pastoral colleagues. I shall always be deeply grateful to God for these years.

I have no doubt that in this book you too will catch a vision of the "One who sits enthroned in heaven", and become convinced that the doctrine of his Sovereignty is no mere academic theory, but rather the bulwark of the lives of his fearful saints, who, fearing him, have "nothing else to fear".

Eric J. Alexander

ACKNOWLEDGEMENTS

For legal reasons, the flyleaf of this book says, "The right of David W Ellis to be identified as the author of this book has been asserted by him." But who can claim such a right? The truth is that a lifetime's input from men and women of God has shaped my understanding of the theology of God's actions in his world. The practical experience of discovering God's hand in those events which impinged on our lives so that we could say there is *Nothing Else to Fear* is indeed personal. But there is more to it than that.

As a family, we have been privileged both to work with and sit under the ministry of many godly colleagues – too many to list. We want to express our sincere gratitude to God for them and all they have taught us. God knows them along with that faithful band of OMF prayer partners who have consistently stood behind us, both on the mission field and now back home in Scotland. The streams of thought shared on the sovereignty of our God as Lord of this Earth have been imbibed through their ministry from God's word.

My deepest thanks must go to my wife Adèle, without whom I would not have dared to write, and to our four boys, John, Mark, Graham and Paul, without whose constant encouragement and massive input this book would never have found its present form.

Finally a word of real appreciation to Professor David Killingray and his wife Margaret who gave up some of their holiday in the Highlands to share their invaluably keen and critical insights on the manuscript, and to Tony Collins of Monarch Books and Sara Foster of OMF for not giving up on me.

My prayer is for a clearer theology of God's ways of acting in his world and for help that we might remain faithful disciples of Christ as we are called to develop a Christian mind-set to face the escalating violence and turmoil of today's world.

David W Ellis
Perth
Scotland
11th September 2003

PLANE WISDOM

The remarkable thing about fearing God is that, when you fear God, you fear nothing else; whereas, if you do not fear God, you fear everything else. (Oswald Chambers)

It was late afternoon in the monsoon season. The air was very humid. Winston, the lanky American pilot, looked impatient. He kept his hand on the door of the small plane as our missionary escort kept talking. Finally, with an eye on the clouds, he insisted that we take off. Now!

The flight was to take us from Miri to one of our mission stations in Lawas. The plane was a single-engined Helio Courier, an unusual machine, able to take off and land on the ultrashort narrow airstrips of rough grass cut into the Borneo jungle. It seemed to have an amazing ability almost to hover as it came in to land at very low speeds. It was ideal for the job.

We had a full load – two other passengers were already sitting patiently waiting. I jumped into the front seat by the pilot and strapped on the harness. The engine roared to life and we rolled down the runway. Back came the yoke and in no time at all we were airborne.

The vista of the jungle, looking like a sea of broccoli laced with yellow brown rivers, stretched below us, and as the altimeter showed us rising above 3,000 feet, we were headed towards a majestic display of massive pillars of white cotton wool clouds. Soon we seemed to be floating in some celestial cathedral as the white columns reached up on either side as far as one could see against the backdrop of a deep blue sky. It looked beautiful. Winston did not share my enthusiasm. I was soon to find out why.

Just how it was that we became enmeshed with those clouds I have forgotten, in the light of what happened next. All I remember was that the more he tried to find a way round them, the more we found ourselves trapped. As the white shroud wrapped itself around us we began to be thrown violently in all directions.

Winston battled with the controls as the violent shaking was accompanied by the sound of what I can only describe as solid chunks of rain battering the windshield. Visibility was non-existent. The blue patches of sky had disappeared.

I looked at the little safety notice pinned to the dashboard in front of me: "No acrobatic spins or turns in this aircraft." I hoped fervently that the engineers who had built this plane had factored a good safety margin into their calculations.

We were somewhere around 4,000 feet up when we went into a steep dive.

"I'm going to try and come down below the weather," Winston explained.

I didn't need too much technology to understand why. The sudden descent was accompanied by vibration, but it smoothed out some of the more violent bumps until, just as we broke out below the cloud, a dark and very solid mass loomed up ahead of us. Winston veered away sharply from the cliff face, but I will never forget what he muttered half under his breath.

"Wow, I wasn't expecting that. Where on earth are we?"

This was not good for the palpitations. Our Malaysian passengers were equally terrified.

The map was spread out on Winston's knees, but since you could hardly see through the water cascading off the screen, there was little point. Thankfully, the plane was now more stable, but clearly we were still lost.

Then Winston flipped a switch by a large circular dial and made various adjustments, until I noticed a red light and heard a series of beeps.

"I'm locking onto the radio beacon from Brunei International Airport," Winston explained. "This is an RDF – the signal will give a bearing we can follow."

The RDF (Radio Direction Finder) had locked onto a beam from the control tower. It steered us north and suddenly there were clear skies and we glimpsed the sea below us. From there it was a fairly simple matter to plot a new course to Lawas.

Finally, Winston nosed the plane over the end of a strip of mown grass which ran through the centre of the mission station, pitched the nose up, landed, and parked the Helio right in front of his house. As his wife ran out to greet us, Winston turned to me and said: "Don't say a word!"

I kept quiet. He didn't want to frighten his wife. Driven off course, lost and overwhelmed by forces he could not control, he confessed to me later that he had been afraid. In all the uncertainties of flying in a hostile environment, his knowledge and respect for the resources that were available to him from outside the situation helped him to handle that fear. His experience and ability to fly by his instruments, and his wisdom in trusting those resources, was the difference between life and death.

As Christians today, it is easy to feel lost and confused by the storms that swirl around us. We are increasingly marginalised. However, God has provided us with resources outside our situation. His word brings objective guidance into our situation and calls us to faith, not fear. Faith and fear oppose one another, and for faith to overcome fear we need to know more of the One in whom our faith is placed.

The fear and anxiety that come from danger or the threat of the unknown are negative. The Bible presents us with a fear that is positive, a fear born of faith. The fear of the Lord is a respect, a reverent awe of God that moves us to live our lives as an open book before him, takes his word seriously and sees doing his will as the most important thing in our lives. It is this fear that brings the confident assurance that God is on our side: "If God is for us, who can be against us?"[1] "He who fears the Lord has a secure fortress, and for his children it will be a refuge."[2]

The book of wisdom, Proverbs, begins by telling us that "the fear of the Lord is the beginning of knowledge",[3] and the philosophical treatise on the empty meaninglessness of living life without God, Ecclesiastes, ends with the same advice: "Here is the conclusion of the matter: fear God and keep his commandments, for this is the whole duty of man."[4]

Only that deep reverence, respect and sense of awe for our God will bring us the assurance of his love and sovereignty in an uncertain world.

Through all the changing scenes of life,
In trouble and in joy,
The praises of my God shall still
My heart and tongue employ.

Of his deliverance I will boast,
Till all that are distressed
From my example comfort take,
And charm their griefs to rest.

O magnify the Lord with me,
With me exalt his Name;
When in distress to him I called,
He to my rescue came.

The hosts of God encamp around
The dwellings of the just;
Deliverance he affords to all
Who on his succour trust.

O make but trial of his love;
Experience will decide
How blest they are, and only they,
Who in his truth confide.

Fear him, ye saints; and you will then
Have nothing else to fear:
Make you his service your delight,
Your wants shall be his care.[5]

Notes

1 Romans 8:31
2 Proverbs 14:26

3 Proverbs 1:7
4 Ecclesiastes 12:13
5 From Psalm 34:1–4, 7–9 by Nahum Tate (1652–1715) and Nicholas Brady (1659–1726), 1696

CHAPTER ONE

NOTHING TO FEAR BUT FEAR

Fear him, ye saints; and you will then
Have nothing else to fear.
(Nahum Tate and Nicholas Brady)

I was in the grip of fear. Smoke, flames, a mob wielding knives
and sticks. A human tidal wave enveloping everything in its
path. There was no escape. I was half a mile from home, trapped
behind the wheel of my car. No way forward. No way back.

The chants of "Allah hu Akbar" were chilling. I could feel
the rush of adrenalin. An estimated mob of around a million
militants was running amok. They had disbanded from a
political rally in central Jakarta, looting and burning like a
swarm of angry locusts, leaving devastation behind them. Our
mission home was in their path.

Instinctively, I pushed the door lock with my elbow and
wound up the window. Smoke from burning shops dimmed
the evening light. Cars and trucks were on fire. Flames roared
from a row of bus windows a few yards from my door.

Youths, shirts tied at the waist, with their headbands making them look like pirates, were rocking the car in front of my bumper. The driver was dragged onto the road.

Then came the sickening thud of hands as my VW Combi began to sway. Angry eyes peered at the windows. Three or four demonstrators hung from the roof gutter. I was next for the "turn and burn" routine. They tried the doors but they were locked. I had seconds.

With clarity born in crisis I sensed, rather than saw, the empty grass verge. Further on, a strip of asphalt led to factory gates: the Coca-Cola plant. The gates were shut. The guards were armed. It was that or nothing.

Letting the clutch in, I shot across the grass. My assailants fell off. But in the half-light of evening the sudden violence of my approach created a problem for the guards. Was this a rioter about to crash the gates? Should they shoot? I screeched to a halt within inches. As I braked, stones were hurled at the van. The truth must have dawned on the gatekeepers. Seeing my white face, they probably mistook me for one of their expat staff. One of the gates was opened just wide enough for me to negotiate the chicane into the factory. I had bought time.

I could see in my mirror guards rushing to lock the gates before the mob entered. There was shooting. I gained as much distance as I could. Parking out of sight behind a large warehouse, I ran inside.

There, in a small room, was a crowd of frightened factory workers huddled together. The heat was oppressive. No electricity, no fans, no light; just a quiet atmosphere of fear. Together, we sat hushed and still in darkness – the air heavy with the unmistakable smell of burning cloves from their kretek cigarettes. How long did we have?

Twilight gave way to darkness. People came and went. An injured man, his left arm slashed and pouring blood, staggered into the room. Immediately, his friends ran to help. It was not clear where he had come from. But as each newcomer arrived they added to the jigsaw of our understanding of what was going on beyond the gates.

I could hardly dare to imagine what must have happened to our offices and mission home. Just half a mile down the road, OMF's mission home stuck out like a sore thumb, a prime target for militants bent on destruction. What if Adèle and all the others had been attacked? I had to get back.

One man came into the room with an air of authority – a factory foreman perhaps? He began to tell us of the shooting and looting he had seen. He seemed so sure that I plucked up courage to ask: "What about Ricoh House?" This was the name given to the buildings next door to our mission home.

"Finished! Burned out! Totally destroyed!"

With the heavy emphasis and explosive syllables of an authentic Javanese speaker, each word sent a shiver down my spine.

Of course I knew I shouldn't be so afraid. I knew chapter and verse by heart. But this was concrete reality. People were being killed. Real blood was being spilled. The sharp cracks were from real rifles. This wasn't TV. It was happening, and I was trapped in it. The irrational mobs were intent on mayhem. And the news that the place where everyone I loved had been destroyed made me sick with fear. How could this be happening and how could God let my family suffer?

It was the same fear I had known some years earlier. Adèle had been very sick. She had tuberculosis and a collapsed lung. I had had to leave her in a hospital in Jogjakarta. Life had become complicated. The communist party was heading towards a coup d'état. They were aggressive. Humanly speaking, we should have left the country when we had been given the opportunity. The British consul had told us to leave but we had a conviction that the Lord wanted us to stay. Now Adèle was in hospital and medicine was hard to get hold of. We were trapped. We could not leave. It was not a simple matter of saying our goodbyes. Getting a government exit permit was complex. And, as we were to discover later when we did try, Indonesian intelligence had a dossier on us. Our prayer partners were not the only ones who had been reading our prayer letters.

The hospital was around 60 miles of pot-holed roads away from our house. I would drive each afternoon on my Vespa and return late at night. Sometimes it was through monsoon rains. And unless you have experienced it, you would never believe how cold that can feel in the tropics.

My guardian angels must have worked overtime. Pot-holes, blinding rain, no gloves, no goggles, and no crash helmet; yet for the two months of commuting I had no accidents. We made new friends, amongst them the kindest of missionaries from a Roman Catholic lay order who day by day visited the hospital and took home Adèle's dirty clothes to wash. They brought her home-made ice cream when the tepid hospital food was hard to swallow.

These missionaries became interested in the all-age Sunday school we taught and soon joined the mailing list for the Bible study materials we produced each week. They then began their own Bible study groups in Jogja. God has ways of surprising us.

Some American friends took pity on us and at a time when Americans were highly unpopular with the communists, they offered me a place to stay in their Agency for International Development (USAID) guest house. From time to time, if I was

tired I would stay overnight rather than negotiate the treach-
erous roads to our village. With the USA at war in Vietnam,
the received wisdom in communist circles was that these good
folk were CIA agents. I will never forget being driven down
the main street underneath a banner which had just been
stretched over the road. It was inscribed with a somewhat
cryptic sample of Indonesian English. It read, "Peace Corps go
to hell from Indonesia."

With laconic humour an American missionary friend said:
"Well, I guess it's probably nearer from here than anywhere
else right now!"

That summed up the climate. In more senses than one, the
writings were on the wall. It was not a good time to be British
or American.

One day on my hospital run, I followed a truck loaded with
a militant communist youth group who were headed in the
same direction. On seeing me, they aimed their slogans
directly at this scooter-riding NEKOLIM – neo-colonial imperialist. It was dusk – the time the insects go walkabout – so
I would smile back as best I could, at the same time having to
spit out the bugs that lodged between my teeth.

Adèle's health was a growing concern. She was losing
weight visibly, and though the doctor was highly competent
and doing all she could, the availability of medicines and suit-
able food was a problem. We shared our concern in a letter
sent to OMF's headquarters in Jakarta. For good measure and
advice we sent a telegram to our mission doctor, Rupert
Clarke, who worked at a hospital in East Java. The letter took
ten days to arrive; the telegram, two weeks. Communication
was difficult. No one had phones. We were isolated. Our one
comfort was to know people back home were praying.

The AID guest house, however, did have a phone. But having grown used to life without a phone, I had almost forgotten what they were for. It was a shock, therefore, within minutes of entering the guest house, to be told I was wanted on the phone. It had to be a mistake. I had never used a phone before in Indonesia. No one knew I was in the house. I did not know anyone who had a phone.

The caller spoke in halting English. Once again the Javanese accent was heavy and menacing: "Mr Ellis, we are coming for you tonight. We know where you are!"

And with that he, whoever he was, was gone. In that climate of fear he did not need to say any more to create panic. Just a week previously, one of the Catholic missionaries had been shot by the communists as he walked home across the paddy fields. Our links with the university and its militant communist Student Movement of Indonesia meant they had a dossier of information on us. Maybe they were suspicious of my regular visits to Jogja. Maybe by staying in the American AID guest house I had confirmed their suspicions. Perhaps I was a CIA agent. Even the missionary who took our wedding photos ended up being charged as a spy for his troubles – previously, he had been a missionary in China and information had been sent to the students by their communist comrades in China. He stood accused of having taken too many photographs! All of us lived with fear in those days.

With Adèle so ill, I could not tell her I was in danger. But I needed to make sure that our papers, which we had to carry everywhere, were safe. I shot off to the hospital and left them in the care of the doctor. She had instructions as to who to contact if anything should happen to me. And with that, I rejoined the three other visitors in the guest house.

They were all UN officials. One of them, a very tall Swedish woman, spoke up, "Don't worry – I will wave my Swedish passport and tell them you are my husband!"

This was kindly meant. The trouble is, in riot situations no one stops to read the fine print. We were all in danger. The US Information Service (USIS) library had been burned down that week. Now it looked as if it was our turn.

I went to my room and prayed as best I could. I decided not to get undressed – after all, if I was going to have to face capture, I had enough British reserve not to relish the thought of being dragged into the street in my pyjamas. So I lay down on the bed. The noise of the night cicadas seemed insistent. It was hot and humid and there were no fans. Sleep would not come.

In the small hours of the morning the noise of the cicadas stopped abruptly. There was a blood-curdling scream. I shot bolt upright. The noise came from outside my window. I peered through the louvres. Two cats were fighting! Little by little my pulse began to slow.

I was still trembling as I knelt down and opened my Bible at Psalm 71:

In thee, O Lord, do I put my trust: let me never be put to confusion. Deliver me in thy righteousness, and cause me to escape: incline thine ear unto me, and save me. Be thou my strong habitation, whereunto I may continually resort: thou hast given commandment to save me; for thou art my rock and my fortress.[1]

"In thee, O Lord, do I put my trust: let me never be put to confusion." That verse had meant so much to me when I first responded to God's call. Slowly, the sense of God's protection became real. I was not alone. There was nothing to fear but fear. I got undressed, lay down and slept. Faith puts on its pyjamas!

God certainly has his "angels unawares". Next morning as I came to breakfast, the house was full of military police: white helmets, Kalashnikovs and machine guns. They had been sent from the local air base while I was sleeping.

The guest house was on the communists' hit-list. Later, we learned that the loyalties of various factions in the airforce were suspect in the political turmoil of those days. Their intelligence had told them of the communist plot. They did not want the guest house to suffer the same fate as the USIS library. They came at dead of night – and we had not sent for them. Mahanaim[2] – the angels of the Lord had camped at that place. Unlikely looking angels, but effective! Words from the old hymn ran through my mind:

> The hosts of God encamp around
> The dwellings of the just;
> Deliverance he affords to all
> Who on his succour trust. . . .
>
> Fear him, ye saints; and you will then
> Have nothing else to fear;
> Make you his service your delight;
> Your wants shall be his care.

But the story has another side. In a small one-roomed apartment on the south-east coast of England a little old lady was at prayer. She was one who spent hours on her knees. A few days after that incident in Jogja, an air letter made its way through the labyrinth of the postal services. At a time when it had taken an internal telegram two weeks to reach our mission doctor and no one had any idea of what we were going through, Miss Evans wrote these words: "The Lord is giving me a great burden of prayer for you. I sense that you are in danger."

The Lord intended to care for and protect us. He put it into the heart of his servant on the other side of the world to pray.

* * *

But this time, as I crouched in the darkness of the Coca-Cola factory, was anybody praying? It was hard to know just what was going to happen. "The hosts of God encamp around the dwellings of the just." But that was not a guarantee of immunity from suffering. What would I do if Adèle had been killed?

I told myself there was nothing to fear but fear, but the knot in my stomach tightened. I had to get back to see for myself – riots or no riots. The van would have to stay. It would probably get stolen or burned, but there was no way to drive through a rioting mob. It would be suicide. If only I wasn't so conspicuous – a large white man was hardly likely to go unnoticed, picking his way through a sea of Asian rioters. But I had to do something. I moved to the door but as I tried to leave, a man stood in the doorway. My way was blocked.

Notes

1 Psalm 71:1–3 (*King James Version*)
2 Genesis 32:1–2

CHAPTER TWO
FROM FEAR TO FAITH

The fear of the Lord is the beginning of wisdom. . . .
Blessed is the man who fears the Lord.[1]

The bed was shaking violently. There was a sound of rumbling. I sat bolt upright. The door burst open and the woven bamboo ceiling was shaking. The light in the middle of the room bobbed up and down like a yo-yo. Both of us leapt out of bed and ran for the courtyard.

All round the yard, doors were opening. Under the clear tropical night a motley group of us stood in night attire, looking sheepish and disorientated. There in the heart of the volcanoes and mountains of West Java we felt very small and utterly helpless. There was nothing we could do. There are no switches to turn off an earthquake. Everything is out of control. At three o'clock in the morning it is hard to think clearly. At the mercy of elemental forces, you are very aware of your mortality. That same knot of fear takes over. You are no longer in control of your environment.

The disciples had had just such an experience. It had been a good day, according to Mark.[2] The crowd at the lakeside were so eager to hear Jesus preach that he had been forced to push off into the lake to get space. He made the boat into his pulpit and spent the day preaching. His disciples basked in the reflected glory of being associated with such a popular teacher. It was a very good day indeed.

In the evening, tired out, Jesus told them to cross the lake to the other side. He then went to sleep on a cushion in the stern of the boat. That was not a problem. The disciples were experienced sailors. They knew the lake. They had crossed it hundreds of times. It was their world.

Fine – at least until, all of a sudden, they hit a storm. The storm was so bad in fact that the waves broke right into the boat. When Matthew tells us the story, he uses the Greek word for an earthquake[3] to describe the storm. This was no ordinary squall. It had such ferocity that these men found themselves at the mercy of elemental forces beyond their ability to control. They were gripped with fear.

After such a good day, it was all the more unexpected. This "earthquake" had a life of its own and it threatened to end theirs. Their sense of panic forced them to wake Jesus. "Don't you care if we drown?" they cried.

Their question, literally, was: "Don't you care if we perish?" They used a strong word, indicating they were convinced that they were about to die. Given the circumstances, they had a point.

Jesus had told them to take him across the lake. Because they had done exactly what he had asked of them, they found themselves in trouble. Clearly, for them, obedience to Jesus was no guarantee of a charmed life without storms. Jesus never promised that for any who follow him. Rather, he spoke more of trouble[4] and persecution. Many faithful followers of Jesus know all about that. He gave no guarantees of prosperity, or freedom from the ills common to humankind. Here on the lake, it was precisely because the disciples had obeyed him that they found themselves in desperate straits.

What happened next can only be described as scary. Jesus stood up and took control of the wind and waves. The implications proved more frightening. The One who was so fully human that he could get worn out and sleep through an earthquake of a storm suddenly showed himself to be the Creator God, able to command the elements. Now that really was terrifying!

Jesus could have ensured that the crossing went smoothly without any storms, but the disciples would have missed out on that revelation of who he was. They would also have failed to learn a vital truth: dictating to God is not faith. "How is it that you have no faith?" he queried.

Maybe they had thought that calling on him was faith. In Matthew's account they seem to be even more demanding. Yet it was not faith that drove them to wake him, but fear. Faith and fear are mutually incompatible, and they needed to understand this.

Jesus asked them why they were fearful[5] – using a word that can mean "timid" or even "cowardly". When the truth as to who he was had dawned, a paradigm shift took place in their thinking. Their fear was overtaken by a sense of terror. Literally, Mark tells us: "They feared a great fear,"[6] which drove them to exclaim: "Who then is this?" They were repeating the rhetorical question from the Old Testament where the writers speak of the Creator God: "Who has gathered up the wind in the hollow of his hands? Who has wrapped up the waters in his cloak. . . . What is his name and the name of his Son?"[7]

No wonder a sense of awe overwhelmed them. They would have been very foolish not to have been afraid. God was standing there before them, and everything else paled into insignificance. Within that greater fear of the Lord they had nothing else to fear but fear.

Mark links the story with the day's preaching when he says that Jesus did not say anything to them without using a parable.[8] This experience was one parable they would never forget. It must have helped to prepare them for that day when another earthquake would strike, and their world would be changed forever.

Jesus' popularity was about to wane. The watershed in his ministry came as Peter made his famous confession. Jesus had asked, "Who do people say the Son of Man is?" Peter had seen who he was: "You are the Christ, the Son of the living God."[9] It was the high point. But from then on, it seemed to be downhill all the way to the "earthquake" of the cross.

So Jesus warned that he must go to Jerusalem and suffer. More than that, he said that "he must be killed and on the third day be raised to life".[10] This was too much for Peter. He took Jesus aside and tried to set him straight. But the path to the cross had been mapped out before the dawn of time. At this moment, however, the disciples had no notion of what was in store.

Naively, they had their own ideas of what Jesus meant when he spoke of establishing his kingdom. Even after his resurrection, their ideas about the kingdom of God were still earthbound, as they asked him: "Lord, are you at this time going to restore the kingdom to Israel?"[11] God's plan and purpose of redemption for the nations had not yet dawned on them. The cross was a great earthquake – unwanted, unexpected, subjecting them to forces over which they had no power.

The cross may have been the first earthquake. But there were to be after-shocks. The religious and political powers that conspired to put Jesus to death now turned their spotlight on his disciples. Peter and John suddenly found themselves in trouble after healing a lame man and causing a general disturbance. They might have felt like crying again: "Lord, don't you care if we perish?"

However, before the Sanhedrin struck, the disciples had experienced a different kind of "earthquake" – Pentecost. The coming of the Holy Spirit had brought their understanding about Jesus into focus. The pages of Scripture came to life and the seemingly random jigsaw of events formed a picture. It was all there in the second psalm. What they were experiencing had been foretold. That realisation was to bring boldness. Peter was so convinced of these truths that he made his controversial claim when he said: "Salvation is found in no one else, for there is no other name under heaven given to men by which we must be saved."[12]

The members of the Sanhedrin were surprised by this display of bold courage: "When they . . . realised that they were unschooled, ordinary men, they were astonished and they took note that these men had been with Jesus."[13] What they had not grasped was that Jesus was still with them, as he had promised to be.[14] Peter and John knew he was with them. So, however fearful they might have been, they remembered with awe the One who commanded the wind and the waves.

In the confidence of his presence with them, they knew there was nothing to fear but fear.

They had moved from fear to faith.

Notes

1 Psalm 111:10 – 112:1
2 Mark 4:35–41
3 Matthew 8:24 σεισμοσ – *an earthquake*
4 John 16:33
5 δειλοσ – *cowardly, timid, fearful*
6 εφοβηθησαν φοβον μεγαν – lit. *feared a great fear*
7 Proverbs 30:4; Psalm 65:7; Psalm 107:25–30 cf. Job 38:4–11; Isaiah 40:12; Job 26:8; 38:8–9
8 Mark 4:34
9 Matthew 16:13–16
10 Matthew 16:21
11 Acts 1:6
12 Acts 4:12
13 Acts 4:13
14 Matthew 28:20

CHAPTER THREE
THE ANTIDOTE TO FEAR

I believe in Christianity as I believe that the sun has risen: not only because I see it, but because by it I see everything else. (C. S. Lewis)

It was Christmas. We were in Central Java. Alongside our work with the Javanese Church, both of us taught at a Christian university. Our students presented us with an unusual Christmas card – a banner strung across the street immediately outside our front gate. Its greeting: "The spirit of Christmas demands that we kick to death all colonial imperialist dogs."

At one end of the bold red lettering stood a crudely painted Union Jack; at the other, the Stars and Stripes. John Bull and Uncle Sam, looking greedy and covered with dollar signs, added an artistic flourish. Not your run of the mill Santa Claus and jingle bells.

This vocabulary was everywhere during the years of President Sukarno's revolution. The banner had been hung there by Christian students from the university. With the inscrutable courtesy of the Javanese, they had asked our permission to put it outside our gate. They were at great pains to assure us it was nothing personal. They did not want us to feel upset.

Poor souls, they had an identity crisis and our presence as Westerners in their university did not help them. We were, after all, representatives from a nation that enjoyed the most hated nation status in their latest propaganda war. It would have been hard for them to understand that perhaps we could feel just a little threatened by their Christmas greetings. But then, we had to try and understand the problem from their point of view. We did what we could, and invited them in for Christmas cake. They left most of it uneaten. Far too sweet by their standards!

The communists were strong. Indonesia, under Sukarno, was pursuing its anti-colonialist revolution. The USA was in Vietnam to the north, and it was an atrocious mess. The so-called "domino theory" predicted that before long, Indonesia would also fall to communism. Any Christian student who did not show enthusiastic support for "the revolution" against colonial imperialists was suspect. So our Christian brothers and sisters had to chant the latest political slogans as loudly as they could, to avoid the accusation of being unpatriotic.

It really looked as if the world's largest Islamic nation was about to turn to communism. Who was to know then that a coup d'état launched by the communist party the following year was to be thwarted? At the time, it was hard not to believe they would succeed. Britain was in the process of helping Malaya, Sarawak and Borneo, along with Singapore, to form a new nation to be called Malaysia. That, in

Indonesian government propaganda, was a neo-colonialist plot orchestrated by Britain to break up the Jakarta–Phnom Penh–Hanoi–Beijing axis of the "New Emerging Forces". As Brits we were not popular.

Nor was our embassy. It stood to one side of a great round-about, opposite the Hotel Indonesia. A great seething mass of humanity gathered there to hurl their insults and demand an audience with the British ambassador.

In his wisdom and years of experience in the diplomatic service, the ambassador realised that he couldn't negotiate with a mob. So he produced his secret weapon – a Scottish soldier, complete with bagpipes.

Our brave Scot was later to be given a medal for his courage for what seemed to us to be nothing but an act of sheer diplomatic folly. He marched up and down in front of the embassy and released all the pent-up power of the pipes. The result was predictable. The rampaging mobs burnt the embassy down. There is a time and place for the pipes – the ramparts of Edinburgh Castle, the mountainside or the city square. But the British embassy in Jakarta, in tropical heat and before rioting mobs, was neither the time nor the place.

I had to go to Jakarta to visit the temporary consulate that replaced the burnt-out embassy. The British ambassador had been withdrawn and a skeleton staff remained. I met the consul. His advice was, in a sentence: "Get out – leave the country!"

I remembered a recent conversation with the principal of the Christian university, in whose house I was living.

"Would you be better off if we left? Are we a danger to you, staying here on campus?"

He had taken his time to answer. When his response came, it was very moving.

"Yes, of course it would be better. Better for you. Better for us. As Christians in Java we have an identity crisis. We are a minority hemmed in by Islam on one side and communism on the other. But you and I are brothers in Christ. You identify with us and take the consequences and we will identify with you. We are members of one family."

Given that bond, my answer to the consul was clear: "Thank you, but we have decided to stay put."

At that, the consul became angry: "When I give advice to businessmen, they follow it. You missionaries give me more trouble than anyone else! You think God will take care of you. Now you are on your own. Is that understood?"

It was. He had a job to do. He was acting in our best interests. We were choosing to ignore his advice. He had to protect himself. We did not blame him. But given the nature of our relationship with the Javanese Church, in Luther's words, it was a case of "Here I stand, I can do no other. So help me God!"

At that point, the BBC Far Eastern service began to send hourly broadcasts to all British citizens in Indonesia. The RAF was sending Hercules aircraft to Jakarta to evacuate all UK citizens. We were told to make our way to the airport and take a plane out to Singapore. It was tempting. Life in Java was far from comfortable, and it was hard not to be fearful.

All day we had been listening to instructions through the BBC as to what we should do. That night it was our weekly prayer meeting and we were working systematically through Isaiah for our Bible readings. High on our agenda as we came to prayer was how we should respond to the advice we were being given. In our Bible readings it "just so happened" that we had come to Isaiah 31.

Woe to those who go down to Egypt for help, who rely on horses, who trust in the multitude of their chariots and in the great strength of their horsemen, but do not look to the Holy One of Israel, or seek help from the LORD. . . . But the Egyptians are men and not God; their horses are flesh and not spirit.[1]

Israel was being warned against a military alliance with Egypt. Egypt had all the latest military equipment by way of fine horses and chariots. It was tempting to place an order. But the message was clear. If Israel put her trust in God he would not let her down. After all, it was God, not the government of Egypt, who was in charge. And it was safer to trust him than to put their confidence in any military alliance.

For us, the message could not have been clearer. Our natural inclination would have been to take up the offer of a free flight to safety. But what could be safer than to be where God had put us? We prayed through the passage. The challenge was to faith, not flight. We were there because we believed God had put us there to do a job. His promise was that he would be with us. We were to stay put. The outcome was in his hands.

Our situation in some respects had parallels with the early church when it found itself in danger from political forces. Persecution had broken out. Peter and John had been hauled before the Sanhedrin. They had been released, but were warned not to preach again in the name of Jesus. This was an order they had no intention of obeying.

They, of course, did not have the temptation of offers from the Royal Air Force. There were no Hercules aircraft to ferry them to safety when the storm of persecution broke out in Jerusalem. Being human, they must have been tempted to run, but they didn't. Instinctively, they knew where to turn.

They prayed their situation into the second psalm. Here they discovered a key to their situation. It helped them to overcome their fearfulness. Despite appearances to the contrary, they were assured that God had not been taken by surprise. Everything was firmly in his control. Luke records:

> On their release, Peter and John went back to their own people and reported all that the chief priests and elders had said to them. When they heard this, they raised their voices together in prayer to God. "Sovereign Lord," they said, "you made the heaven and the earth and the sea, and everything in them. You spoke by the Holy Spirit through the mouth of your servant, our father David:
>
>> 'Why do the nations rage and the peoples plot in vain?
>> The kings of the earth take their stand and the rulers gather together against the Lord and against his Anointed One.'
>
> Indeed Herod and Pontius Pilate met together with the Gentiles and the people of Israel in this city to conspire against your holy servant Jesus, whom you anointed. They did what your power and will had decided beforehand should happen. Now, Lord, consider their threats and enable your servants to speak your word with great boldness. Stretch out your hand to heal and perform miraculous signs and wonders through the name of your holy servant Jesus."[2]

Peter's fearless statement to the members of the Sanhedrin that he had healed the man in the name of Jesus Christ of Nazareth "whom you crucified" had done little to endear him to them. They could have had Peter crucified there and then, and he knew it. Yet, fearlessly, he went on to say to them: "Salvation is found in no one else, for there is no other name under heaven given to men by which we must be saved."[3] His head was fair and square on the chopping block. But what this psalm taught the young church was that it was God, not kings and rulers or any members of the Sanhedrin, who was controlling the situation.

"Faith is being sure of what we hope for and certain of what we do not see."[4] Their faith was evident in that they saw what others could not see. Soaked as they were in God's word, they knew, despite all appearances to the contrary, that their God was the "Sovereign Lord". That governed their reaction in the hour of crisis and gave them confident assurance. They were in safe hands.

Even the cross, which at the time had seemed to be an unspeakable tragedy, was something God had planned from all eternity. For Jesus was "the Lamb that was slain from the creation of the world".[5] As Peter had said at Pentecost: "This man was handed over to you *by God's set purpose and fore-knowledge*; and you, with the help of wicked men, put him to death by nailing him to the cross."[6] That truth now reassured them as they prayed on: "They did what your power and will had decided beforehand should happen." It was not that God sanctioned the evil done to his Son, but in his sovereignty even the deeds of those evil men had been taken into account in the outworking of his purposes for redemption. The most criminal miscarriage of justice of all time, clear evidence of the rebellion of kings and rulers, would not have the last word.

By faith, they could see beyond the world of time and space. That was more important than anything they were experiencing at that moment in Jerusalem. What they saw by faith was that the psalm went beyond any historical incident. Here was truth with a universal and eternal significance. God is establishing his kingdom on earth. The fact that the world stands in rebellion against that kingdom was known before time began. We need to grasp that perspective today.

It is not our politicians and presidents who control the destiny of our world, but our Sovereign Lord. He has his own agenda and is moving everything inexorably towards that day when "the earth will be filled with the knowledge of the glory of the Lord, as the waters cover the sea".[7]

That message runs through Scripture to the very last book, Revelation. There the curtains are drawn back to show us a throne at the heart of the universe. God is on that throne. He rules, and that rule encompasses even the chaos we see in the nations around us today. The truth is, as expressed by another of the psalms: "The Lord reigns, let the nations tremble; he sits enthroned between the cherubim, let the earth shake. Great is the Lord in Zion; he is exalted over all the nations."[8]

Chapters 4 and 5 of Revelation describe that throne. For John, incarcerated for his faith on the barren rock of an island called Patmos, that vision was meant to be an encouragement. But John sees a problem. Something is wrong. There is a scroll in God's hand. But for reasons John cannot understand, it remains sealed. It seems that no one is qualified or able to open the scroll or to look inside. That brings tears to John's eyes. Is the occupant of the throne unable to rule and does that mean John is left at the mercy of evil powers?

The tears vanish as he hears that "the Lion of the tribe of Judah, the Root of David, has triumphed. He is able to open the scroll and its seven seals."[9] He looks up, expecting to see a lion, but instead he sees "a Lamb, looking as if it had been slain, standing in the centre of the throne".[10] And he knows, better than anyone, that this lamb bearing the marks of his slaughter is none other than Jesus, the Anointed One, his Lord and Saviour. This is the One who, after his resurrection, had said to him: "All authority in heaven and on earth has been given to me. Therefore go and make disciples of all nations."[11]

John sees who is shaping history. He sees the One who is in charge, even of his suffering in prison. It is the Lord and his Anointed One who will bring everything to that great climax when all the nations will bow and every tongue will confess Jesus Christ to be Lord.[12]

The universe is governed by the throne. Everything must be seen from that viewpoint. Nothing is excluded from God's rule. And when all hell seems to break loose around us we may feel fearful, but it is God, not the devil nor the powers of evil abroad in the world, whom we are to fear.

The devil wants us to fear him. He is delighted if we think of him in equal terms with God. The scale of his deception is enormous. He is out to get us to attribute to him God-like powers that he does not possess. He is, after all, "the father of lies".[13]

Thanks to *Star Wars*, many of us view the devil as if he were "the dark side of the force" – God's opposite. That is exactly the blasphemous claim Satan wants us to believe. God has no opposites. God is unique. As C. S. Lewis said in the preface to his *Screwtape Letters*:

The commonest question is whether I really "believe in the Devil". Now, if by "the Devil" you mean a power opposite to God and, like God, self-existent from all eternity, the answer is certainly No. There is no uncreated being except God. God has no opposite. No being could attain a "perfect badness" opposite to the perfect goodness of God; for when you have taken away every kind of good thing (intelligence, will, memory, energy, and existence itself) there would be none of him left.

The proper question is whether I believe in devils. I do. That is to say, I believe in angels, and I believe that some of these, by the abuse of their free will, have become enemies to God and, as a corollary, to us. These we may call devils. They do not differ in nature from good angels, but their nature is depraved. Devil is the opposite of angel only as Bad Man is the opposite of Good Man. Satan, as the leader or dictator of devils, is the opposite, not of God, but of Michael.

Satan is a formidable enemy. We must never underestimate him. But the fear of God is the beginning of wisdom and knowledge,[14] not a preoccupation with the devil and the powers of evil.

Jesus emphasised that truth when he said that we were not to "be afraid of those who kill the body and after that can do no more". Rather he told us in the strongest possible terms who it is we are to fear – "I will show you whom you should fear: Fear him who, after the killing of the body, has power to throw you into hell. Yes, I tell you, fear him."[15] And to underline that same truth, Jesus called himself "the stone the builders rejected" and gave us this warning: "Everyone who falls on that stone will be broken to pieces, but he on whom it falls will be crushed."[16]

Godly fear is our one true hope, and the antidote to fearfulness.

Notes

1 Isaiah 31:1–3
2 Acts 4:23–30

3 Acts 4:12
4 Hebrews 11:1
5 Revelation 13:8
6 Acts 2:23
7 Habakkuk 2:14
8 Psalm 99:1–2
9 Revelation 5:5
10 Revelation 5:6
11 Matthew 28:18–19
12 Philippians 2:8–11
13 John 8:44
14 Proverbs 9:10 and 1:7
15 Luke 12:4, 5
16 Luke 20:18

CHAPTER FOUR

THE FEAR BEYOND TERROR

... disillusioned, and not a moment too soon. (C. S. Lewis)

I watched the bubbles. Normally, bubbles rise. These were falling. Closer and closer they travelled down the tube. I thought there weren't supposed to be any bubbles in an intravenous drip. Guiltily, they scurried out of sight through the Ventlon in the back of my hand. They were inside – somewhere.

Questions, stimulated by fever, tumbled around my mind. Aren't you supposed to make sure there aren't any bubbles? Did the nurse not see them when she changed the drip? How many bubbles could you get into your veins before a clot formed? The man in the bed next to me has a deep vein thrombosis. Did he get too much air into his veins?

I had driven myself to hospital after battling to preach through the pain barrier at a church in London. By the time I arrived at the hospital, the pain had become intense. Several years of violent dysentery in Java had done little to help my

43

digestive system. Now a serious intestinal infection was threatening to require major surgery. I was in considerable discomfort as I lay in the hospital ward – the "why" and the "what if" questions never far from my mind. It was hard not to be fearful.

Suddenly an animated nurse burst into the ward.

"Switch on the TV! Something's happening in New York!"

It was September 11th 2001. All eyes in the ward focused on the screen. Who could forget where they were when those first images ploughed into our minds? Tied by an intravenous drip to a hospital bed, I was a captive audience. The bubbles were forgotten. My "whys" and "what ifs" faded into insignificance. This was big. The world had changed. As the horror of it all began to sink in, any fears I had felt for myself moved to a different plane. Where was God when all this was happening?

"The Day that Changed the Modern World" was how one newspaper headline summed it all up. But the world did not change. We did. Our perspective changed. Our eyes opened to reality. The world had declared its colours.

Ever since Adam chose to ignore his Maker's directions, evil has been present in our world. Like the cancer it is, evil does not discriminate. Its nature is to attack and destroy wherever and whenever it can.

In the dark days of 1939 when Hitler's armies raped Poland, the world plunged into the horrors of the Second World War. At that time, C. S. Lewis delivered an address to the students of Oxford University at the Church of St Mary. The text of that message became known as "Learning in Wartime". In the light of all that is happening today, it has contemporary relevance:

I think it is important to see the present calamity in a true perspective. The war creates no absolutely new situation; it simply aggravates the permanent human situation so that we can no longer ignore it. Human life has always been lived on the edge of a precipice. . . . We are mistaken when we compare war with "normal life". Life has never been normal . . .

War makes death real to us: and that would have been regarded as one of its blessings by most of the great Christians of the past. They thought it good for us to be always aware of our mortality. I am inclined to think they were right. All the animal life in us, all schemes of happiness that centred in this world, were always doomed to a final destruction. In ordinary times only a wise man can realise it. Now the stupidest of us knows. We see unmistakably the sort of universe in which we have all along been living, and must come to terms with it. If we had foolish un-Christian hopes about human culture, they are now shattered. If we thought we were building up a heaven on earth, if we looked for something that would turn the present world from a place of pilgrimage into a permanent city satisfying the soul of man, we are disillusioned, and not a moment too soon.

In the aftermath of September 11th and the declaration of the so-called "War on Terror", how can we as believers be helped "to see the present calamity in a true perspective"? How can we say to our fearfulness that God is still in charge?

Immediately, we face a fact that may seem both uncomfortable and unpalatable. If, as Scripture teaches, God is the Sovereign Lord of history, it follows that this world is not at the mercy of blind fate. The logic of that statement is clear. The devastation of the World Trade Centre happened, and God did not intervene to stop it. He was not taken by surprise. He allowed it to happen. That may offend what someone has described as "the soft edges of our post-modern spirituality". It certainly challenges a popularly held view of God.

More than a decade ago the Berlin Wall fell. The bankruptcy of atheistic communism was exposed, and the West rejoiced. After all, in our book, communism was "evil". Smugly, we congratulated ourselves that our democracies were "good". God, we said, was doing a new thing among the nations. The Sovereign Lord of history was on the move. And all the time, underlying our words was an unspoken conviction that God must be "on our side". We are good – they are bad.

But what are we to say now? If God is on our side, how could he allow us to experience such suffering and devastation? What will the repercussions be from this War on Terror? It is a question that raises more questions than answers, and a problem to which many offer their opinions.

When on my hospital bed, I heard one TV commentator say, "Just think of it, the two symbols of our power and prosperity destroyed in one hour!" I wondered if he was consciously echoing the lament of the world's politicians as they witness the fall of Babylon in the book of Revelation. There, it is reported that world leaders, seeing the smoke rising from the ruins, cry out: "Woe! Woe, O great city, O Babylon, city of power! In one hour your doom has come!"

Was our TV commentator aware that in the aftermath of Babylon's doom, the great lament of the politicians would soon be joined by the businessmen as the stock market plunged?

> Woe! Woe, O great city, dressed in fine linen, purple and scarlet, and glittering with gold, precious stones and pearls! . . . In one hour such great wealth has been brought to ruin!

Did he sense the impact this might have on the airlines and shipping companies as they joined in the chorus?

> ... All who travel by ship, the sailors, and all who earn their living from the sea, will stand far off. When they see the smoke of her burning, they will exclaim, "Was there ever a city like this great city?" They will throw dust on their heads, and with weeping and mourning cry out: "Woe! Woe, O great city, where all who had ships on the sea became rich through her wealth! In one hour she has been brought to ruin!"[1]

The story of Babylon starts with the infamous tower of Babel.[2] The biblical significance of that first reference is hard to miss. Ronald Youngblood has written: "At Babel rebellious man undertook a united and godless effort to establish for himself, by a titanic human enterprise, a world renown by which he would dominate God's creation." So Babylon in all its proud luxury and glory, throughout Scripture, comes to signify a culture of rebellion that puts its faith into its own efforts and stands in defiance against God; a kingdom that attempts by human effort to seize control of history.

In their pursuit of materialistic values the economists and businessmen, along with the rest of us – the "bodies and souls of men"[3] – are all entangled in the octopus-like tentacles of Babylon. Yet as history is drawn to a climax with the second coming of Christ, this proud, materialistic, self-sufficient culture will be shown to be bankrupt and ultimately destroyed.[4] "In one hour", Babylon, all that symbolises the kingdom of man and his godless values, is to be thrown down. Then heaven will declare: "The kingdom of the world has become the kingdom of our Lord and of his Christ, and he will reign for ever."[5] Was September 11th a warning shot across our bows?

Now it would be a gross mistake to single out any one country and identify it with Babylon. That would be to miss the deeper significance of biblical truth and repeat the same mistakes that have marked numerous attempts throughout church history to identify Babylon with the latest bête noire. Babylon is neither America nor Great Britain nor Russia, nor Iraq nor anywhere else. Babylon is any man-made value system that defies the rule of God. In that sense, Babylon manifests itself in the culture of each and every nation. It is the manifestation of godlessness on a worldwide scale.

That there are clear parallels with the symbolism of the book of Revelation should come as a warning. The spirit of Babylon is in all our hearts and the cultures from which we come. By putting our faith in ourselves, and our own achievements, we defy the rule of God's kingdom. All this happened in New York, a city that, with some justification, calls itself "the world's capital". It has given up some of its precious land to house the United Nations. It has great wealth and prosperity. It has become the major hub of the world's economy, sophisticated and prosperous. It has many remarkable achievements, not least of which is its ability to communicate instantly with the whole world.

From my hospital bed I witnessed the horrors of 9/11 within minutes of it taking place. Had it happened in some corner of the Third World we might never have heard of it at all. The trumpet has sounded a message loud and clear, and none of us can say we have not heard it. World Babylon has been warned. A day is coming when it will be thrown down as Christ comes to reign. In the words of Joachim Neander's hymn:

> Human pride and earthly glory,
> Sword and crown betray his trust;
> What with care and toil we fashion,
> Tower and temple, fall to dust;
> But God's power,
> Hour by hour
> Is my temple and my tower.

But if this is a universal message for the whole world, does it have a special added significance for those of us living in the comfortable prosperity of our Western democracies? If the Sovereign Lord of history exposed the bankruptcy of atheistic communism, might he not now be exposing to us the bankruptcy of all that we in the West have come to see as so basic to "our way of life"? Ours is a way of life that is marked by practical atheism. Difficult and unpleasant though the thought may be, has God used terrorists to wake us up to the nature of our rebellion? Does he want to warn us about the bankruptcy and evil of our society? This isn't exactly what we expected him to do after the collapse of the Berlin Wall. We may have to re-evaluate our understanding of his ways.

In C. S. Lewis's *The Lion, The Witch and The Wardrobe*, one of the four children at the Beavers' house said that she would feel nervous about meeting the lion, Aslan. Mrs Beaver said:

> "That you will, dearie, and no mistake . . . if there's anyone who can appear before Aslan without their knees knocking, they're either braver than most or else just silly."
>
> "Then he isn't safe?" said Lucy.
>
> "Safe?" said Mr Beaver; "don't you hear what Mrs Beaver tells you? Who said anything about safe? 'Course he isn't safe. But he's good. He's the king, I tell you."

The prophet Habakkuk in the Old Testament knew all about knees knocking. He had been on his knees praying for revival, sickened by the godless state of his nation. But God's answer was not what he bargained for. As he got up, his knees were most certainly knocking. His nation was in for a dreadful shock:

> Look at the nations and watch – and be utterly amazed. For I am going to do something in your days that you would not believe, even if you were told. I am raising up the Babylonians, that ruthless and impetuous people . . .[6]

That was certainly not the answer he wanted or expected. It was terrifying. God was about to bring judgement on his people. God had answered his prayer in the depths, not the shallows. And as the truth of God's answer sank in, Habakkuk was appalled:

> O Lord, you have appointed them to execute judgment; O Rock, you have ordained them to punish.[7]

The more he thought about it, the more he had a theological problem. How could a holy God use the treachery of the evil Babylonian warriors whom he viewed to be terrorists, to deal with his own people, who were nowhere near as evil as the Babylonians? Habakkuk cries out in protest:

> Your eyes are too pure to look on evil; you cannot tolerate wrong. Why then do you tolerate the treacherous? Why are you silent while the wicked swallow up those more righteous than themselves?[8]

God's answer leaves as much unanswered as it answers. But one thing becomes crystal clear. Those who, like the Babylonians, resort to evil will in turn be consumed by the evil they choose to use. Terry Waite, former adviser to the Archbishop of Canterbury and for several years a hostage of Islamic militants in Lebanon, said, "The terrible thing about terrorism is that ultimately it destroys those who practise it. Slowly but surely, as they try to extinguish life in others, the light within them dies." Evil is true to its nature – it destroys. At the same time, evil always exposes itself to the ultimate judgement of God. God sets its bounds.

Despite the evil, God remains holy and Habakkuk is called to hold onto the ultimate righteousness and goodness of God. That said, he feels he has no line to fathom why God would allow evil men to wreak havoc on his nation. In their arrogance they have made evil a way of life. Habakkuk, in sharp contrast, comes to understand that "the righteous will live by his faith".[9] So it is by that faith that he clings to what he knows of God, in the face of everything that seems contradictory: "O Lord, are you not from everlasting? My God, my Holy One, we will not die."[10]

He recognises that God is still on the throne: "But the Lord is in his holy temple; let all the earth be silent before him."[11]

In faith he affirms that ultimately a day will come when "the earth will be filled with the knowledge of the glory of the Lord, as the waters cover the sea".[12]

In recognition of what is about to happen in his land he prays fervently, "Lord . . . I stand in awe of your deeds . . . in wrath remember mercy."[13]

Habakkuk's final affirmation of faith shows us the mindset we need to cultivate in the face of terror.

I heard and my heart pounded, my lips quivered at the sound; decay crept into my bones, and my legs trembled. Yet I will wait patiently for the day of calamity to come on the nation invading us. Though the fig tree does not bud and there are no grapes on the vines, though the olive crop fails and the fields produce no food, though there are no sheep in the pen and no cattle in the stalls, yet I will rejoice in the Lord, I will be joyful in God my Saviour. The Sovereign Lord is my strength; he makes my feet like the feet of a deer, he enables me to go on the heights.[14]

Living in the southern kingdom of Judah, Habakkuk knew that Israel in the north had faced judgement when she ignored her role as God's servant. God had called his people to be salt and light to the nations. He had given them many warnings.

Israel failed. Instead of bearing witness to God's glory, she gave herself to the formal rituals of religion and the worship of other gods. The testimony was distorted and the light died. The prophet Hosea warned that by their disobedience they were sowing the wind and would "reap the whirlwind".[15]

That whirlwind came with the Assyrian conquest. God called these Assyrians "the rod of my anger, in whose hand is the club of my wrath".[16] The warning ignored, the northern kingdom disappeared. To this day, the people of that region are remembered as the ten lost tribes of Israel. This is a warning and example we should not ignore.

Jesus made it equally clear to us that we are to be salt and light. He commissioned us to make disciples of all nations. The moral decay in our own Western society begs the question: how effective are we? The voice of Christian conscience is all but silent in the places of power. The world knows more of the commercial enterprises and moral depravity of the West than the gospel. Apart from a few committed individuals, the missionary vision of the Western church and its support for overseas missions has been eclipsed by a preoccupation with its own interests.

We must not ignore Peter's warning ". . . it is time for judgment to begin with the family of God; and if it begins with us, what will the outcome be for those who do not obey the gospel of God?"[17] As followers of Christ, recent events should call us to repentance and a missionary concern for the world around.

Our knees may knock as we think of all that is happening but our faith needs the confidence expressed in Joachim Neander's hymn:

> All my hope on God is founded,
> All my trust he shall renew,
> He, my guide through changing order,
> Only good and only true:
> God unknown,
> He alone
> Calls my heart to be his own.

Only then will we begin "to see the present calamity in a true perspective".

Notes

1 Revelation 18:16–19
2 Genesis 11:1ff.
3 Revelation 18:13
4 Revelation 17–19
5 Revelation 11:15

 6 Habakkuk 1:5–6
 7 Habakkuk 1:12b
 8 Habakkuk 1:13
 9 Habakkuk 2:4b
10 Habakkuk 1:12
11 Habakkuk 2:20
12 Habakkuk 2:14
13 Habakkuk 3:2
14 Habakkuk 3:16–19
15 Hosea 8:7
16 Isaiah 10:5
17 1 Peter 4:17

CHAPTER FIVE

NOT RELIGION BUT REPENTANCE

Who among us is willing to destroy a piece of their own heart? (Alexander Solzhenitsyn)

The man barring my way as I made to escape from that dark room during those riots in Jakarta was a Muslim. He had the air of someone who expected to be obeyed. He wore the little white hat that indicated he had made the pilgrimage to Mecca – he was a Hajji. He was serious about his religion. Outside, his people were rioting.

Yet I was determined to get out. I moved to the door but as I made to go past him, he shot out a hand and grabbed my arm. His grip was firm but kindly. Aware of my fear, he spoke softly. "Don't be afraid! Stay still. It's not time yet. Later – I will go with you. Patience, Tuan."

I deferred. It meant another two hours – an eternity. I talked with the others around the room. They were every bit as afraid as I was. They discovered that I was a missionary – there are no secrets in Asia. I was the only Christian in a room full of

Muslims, and they were as kind and polite as they could be. Their concern for what might have happened to my family was genuine. Circumstances had thrown us together. We found a common bond.

Gradually, the noises on the street quietened. My Hajji friend slipped out of the room to see if the coast was clear. A few minutes later he returned and beckoned. Then, in the way Indonesian men seem able to hold another man's hand without embarrassment, he gripped my hand and just held on. Hand in hand, we stepped out into the tropical night.

Our path was lit by flames from the burning vehicles. The air was full of the acrid smell of burning rubber. But it felt fresh after that stuffy room. We crossed the yard to thread our way through the shadowy back streets of the housing estate, past the Muslim hospital and finally out onto the main road. Rioters were still wandering around with sticks, prodding at burning vehicles. Skirting a fence, we moved towards a pyre of burning cars and buses. They were to the side of the mission home. No wonder our foreman thought the buildings had been burned out and destroyed. From the road, that is certainly how it looked. I felt utterly devastated and hollow.

The burning vehicles created a sense of confusion. Yet, as my eyes adjusted to the smoke and flames, I saw that, far from being illuminated, the mission home had all but disappeared from sight. The lights were off. One of the missionaries was standing at the gate. But there was something else. In the darkness, the glare of light from the burning vehicles flickered on the trees in the garden. And the eye was deceived. A curtain of light seemed to hide the building. Unless you knew it to be there, it was almost invisible. By the grace of God, the mobs had ignored it and gone to loot the lucrative shops next door. Adèle was safe, along with all the other missionaries. They had gathered to pray, and their prayers had been answered.

It was a scary time. Elections were two weeks away. Extremists were bent on chaos. As people walked down the street they would be confronted by militant fanatics who would challenge them to vote for their party. When a knife is pressed against your throat there is little time to argue about the finer points of politics. Some of our Indonesian colleagues had terrifying experiences.

But that night, identified in fear with a frightened group of Muslims hiding in the warehouse, I was given a lot to think about. They showed me concern and compassion. One of them even risked his life for a total stranger and a foreigner whose religion was different from his.

My Muslim guide came right into the house. He didn't let go of my hand until he could pass it over to Adèle. He took a quick drink of tea and then, when we sought to reward him in some way for bringing me home through the riots, he refused. Slipping quietly out through the darkness of our garden into the light of the burning vehicles next door, he disappeared and was gone. He was a Muslim, a Hajji at that. To me, he had been an angel unawares.

To think that Muslims are bad because they follow the religion of Islam with all its political connotations is naive. Sadly, religion wears many masks. As the sectarian conflict in Northern Ireland has shown us, some evil men will shelter under a mask of Protestantism while others will call themselves Catholic. The Bible reminds us that it is the heart which is evil and desperately wicked.[1] A wicked heart can hide behind any religious mask.

Once, with a group of missionaries going to a conference in West Java, we found ourselves in a horrendous traffic jam. We were part of a slurry of vehicles all trying to edge forwards and sideways, jostling around in a desperate attempt to get through the narrow toll gate to the motorway. In and out of this mêlée, salesmen and beggars flitted from car to car. Little boys threatened to clean windscreens – a proven way of etching the dust into the glass. It was hard to believe the pandemonium. Harder still, perhaps, to realise that you could get used to it to such an extent that when people back home grumble about a traffic snarl-up on the motorway you wonder what they have to complain about!

But that day it wasn't just the traffic. Weaving in and out of the waiting cars were figures dressed in the hooded white robes of Muslim martyrs, their faces hidden. They were Laskar Jihad – "Soldiers of the Jihad". Carrying collection boxes, they moved from vehicle to vehicle. Whether from fear or sympathy for the cause, drivers stuffed mangled rupiah notes into their boxes. They were collecting for the holy war against Christians in the Moluccas. At the time, according to a BBC article, some 10,000 people had been slaughtered in Ambon and the Moluccan islands. Thousands more had been driven from their homes and had fled as refugees to other islands. We had to withdraw our missionaries to the relative safety of Java.

I wondered what we would do when these Laskar Jihad came to us. Mercifully, whether by intention or discretion, they passed by as if we didn't exist. It was unnerving. These were not people I would want to meet again – as different from my devout Muslim friend at the Coca-Cola factory as darkness and light.

Today we watch as two of the world's major religions, Islam and Christianity, view each other through their own set of distorting mirrors, locked on a collision course in a conflict which has lasted for centuries. Two religions with opposing worldviews confronting and defying one another: this is a situation the devil is more than happy to exploit. Religion provides useful camouflage.

"Religion" is not a word the Bible treats with great sympathy. Jesus reserved his fiercest denunciations for the hypocrisy of "religion". It was "religion" that called for his death. What God looks for is not religion but a personal, living relationship with him. He neither wants nor needs "religion".

A living relationship with God is what being a Christian is all about. It begins with God, not us. He takes the initiative. He is the author of our faith and even when we were his enemies he came to us in his Son.[2] The central reality of our faith is not the church and its organisation but the living Christ – the Word who became flesh and lived among us – God the Son who could say with authority, "I am the way and the truth and the life. No one comes to the Father except through me."[3]

None of us can climb up to God. God came to us when Jesus came to our world. The angel said when he was about to be born: ". . . they will call him 'Immanuel' – which means 'God with us'".[4] Christianity at its core is not a religion; Christianity is Christ.

Jesus, and a living relationship with him, is central. While we may have questions about aspects of Karl Barth's theology, I believe he was right when he made the daring statement in his *Church Dogmatics* that "religion is unbelief . . . [and] . . . the one great concern of godless man".

That statement seems to be a contradiction. The point is, however, that "religion" is something we create as human beings. Like those who built the tower of Babel, "religion" is our human attempt to construct a way to God, a DIY human system of beliefs and rituals. As such it comes from earth, not heaven. It is a secular phenomenon, not a living faith. It follows therefore that among followers of any religion, there will be those who are "good" and those who are "evil". In those situations where religion is wedded closely to politics the mix is dangerous.

My barber in Sevenoaks, in Kent, who had the unenviable task of trying to discover which hairs to cut and which to leave on my bald pate, used to say, "I always avoid discussing matters of religion or politics." It was patently untrue. He loved to talk politics. He did it all the time. But knowing where I was coming from as a missionary, he was anxious to head me off from any embarrassing discussion about faith. He separated religion from politics – something we Westerners may do, but something a Muslim would never think of doing. For Muslims, religion and politics are one. They do not distinguish.

This means that for Muslims the government of their land should be religious, not secular. The fact that some Islamic countries do have secular governments is usually a legacy from the years of colonial rule. Fundamentally in Islam, culture, politics and religion are not labelled into separate compartments. Islamic law is not limited to matters of personal faith and practice, but covers legislation for civil life, family matters, constitutional and criminal affairs. That is why, when Western models of secular government came to be installed in some Islamic countries, radical Muslims felt that their leadership had been emasculated.

Since many Muslims identify politics with lifestyle, the more radical elements of Islam identify the lifestyle and politics of the Western world with its professed religion, Christianity. We may protest that our Western culture and what it means to be a Christian are two different things, but that does not always register in their thinking.

If we compare what it means to be born again and saved by God's grace with the religion of Islam, we are not comparing like with like. Jesus said, "My kingdom is not of this world."[5] Muhammad would never have said that. He saw his kingdom as being very much of this world. When Jesus looked at a coin and said, "Give to Caesar what is Caesar's, and to God what is God's",[6] Muhammad would not have agreed. For Islam, to quote Islamologist Professor Bernard Lewis, "Caesar and God are one." That is why, for Islam, political protest finds religious expression, and religious protest finds political expression. Islam embraces both a political and a social order. It has a clear missionary vision – to bring the whole world under Islamic law.

As believers, we would distance ourselves from the secularism and godlessness of our Western culture. But that is not easy for our Muslim friends to understand. The hedonistic lifestyle of the West they would identify with our beliefs – an identification that puts tremendous pressure on those Christians who live in largely Muslim communities. Christian believers in Muslim lands, by association with the corruption of the West, are sometimes tragically misunderstood and persecuted as a result. In Indonesia, for instance, to purge their land of such corruption, fanatical Muslim activists have targeted Christian communities, bombed their churches, and forced many to convert to Islam at the point of the sword. The so-called "Bali bomb" in 2002 which killed so many Western holidaymakers in a night club followed a series of incidents in night clubs and bars in Jakarta over the years, in which radical Islam has sought to destroy what it viewed simplistically as evidence of the godless hedonism of the West and its Christian religion.

One day, the Scottish poet Robert Burns was sitting comfortably in church. He was behind a pious lady who was wearing a bonnet trimmed beautifully with ribbons and bows. He was fascinated. Then suddenly, crawling through the decorations he saw one of her head lice. He was struck by the sheer incongruity of it all – the demure lady, prim and proper sitting piously in church, totally oblivious of the louse on her bonnet. Little could she have known that one of her head lice would give birth to some of his most famous lines:

> O wad some Power the giftie gie us
> To see oursels as ithers see us!
> It wad frae monie a blunder free us,
> An' foolish notion.

Burns probably found the incongruity of the louse more interesting than the sermon, but through his art a sermon lives on.

If we want to avoid "monie a blunder" in our relationship with Muslims we need to understand how they view the "Christian" bonnet that adorns our heads. As they see us, the ribbons and lace are crawling alive with all the lice of Western immorality – not a pretty sight.

The evil one is a master at getting Islam to concentrate on the lice or what they interpret to be the lice. It is a small step from that to persuade some Muslims into believing they must do some delousing to avoid becoming infected themselves! The devil "prowls around like a roaring lion looking for someone to devour".[7] His objective is the downfall of the kingdom of God. If there are followers of any religion who are willing to bend to his purpose he will use them. From the hyper-religious Pharisees to modern Islamic militants, religious extremists have co-operated well with him. He is not fussy. Any religion will do.

His strategy is to trick such people into thinking they are acting in the name of God, and for righteous ends. He has had considerable success in the West. We have a great deal of unsavoury junk in our backyard. Terror is not the exclusive weapon of 21st century Islamic militants. There is much blood on our hands. Jesus said: "Why do you look at the speck of sawdust in your brother's eye and pay no attention to the plank in your own eye?"[8] He did not tell us we were to ignore the sawdust in our brother's eye but he wanted us, first of all, to check out the plank! You don't have 20-20 vision when there is a plank in your eye. Seeing evil in others is something we are good at. It makes us feel better. As the American author Norman Mailer put it: "If you're half-evil, nothing soothes you more than to think the person you are opposed to is totally evil."

And were those young men who crashed into the Twin Towers in New York totally evil? What drove them to pay the ultimate price for what they believed in? Were they mad? Far from it. As Charles Krauthammer said the day after the disaster: "This is a formidable enemy. To dismiss it as a bunch of 'cowards' perpetuating 'senseless acts of violence' is complacent nonsense. People willing to kill thousands of innocents while they kill themselves are not cowards. They are deadly vicious warriors and need to be treated as such."

An honest look at how many Muslim folk may perceive the lice crawling on the bonnet of our Christianity in the West is sobering. From the notorious Crusades to our imperialist expansion over the past two centuries, they can only see the record as evil. Doubtless in this fallen world some aggressive colonial policies were hijacked by evil. You do not need to look far back in history to see the scars.

On the other hand, not all colonial history was bad. Without it, much of the world could still be living in the Middle Ages. It depends on who is viewing the facts.

As Muslim radicals see it, European armies marched for their own commercial and political interest into Indonesia, Malaya, India, Egypt, North Africa and the Middle East. The Europeans fought their people, conquered their lands, and removed their leaders.

They accuse the West of terror, persecution, ethnic cleansing and the substitution of secular laws for the Shariah – Islamic law. The division between civil and religious government led to the enfeebling of their peoples. Their economies became dominated by the West, the result being to create a sense of inferiority. Western technology has threatened their cultural values and robbed them of self-respect.

This perspective helps to explain why some Muslims would identify the secular society of the West with what they see to be its religion. Whatever the true facts, in their book, Christians must shoulder a fair share of the blame. Imperialism has sown the wind. Through recent acts of terror Muslim radicals have served notice that they intend it to reap the whirlwind.

From time to time, history has seen the rise of radical Muslim leaders with a vision to revive the pride and spirit of their faith. To the West they have appeared to be guerrillas and terrorists. But to the faithful they were charismatic leaders seeking revival. In that sense, Osama bin Laden comes from a long succession of radicals who have fought to restore the self-worth and pride of Islam.

The Second World War brought a dramatic change in the world order. The Allies may have won the war in Europe and Asia, but the Western colonial states lost their empires. Two new superpowers, the USA and the USSR, emerged and the age of Western imperialism appeared to be coming to an end. A new era was dawning in which those who felt themselves to have been oppressed could set out with a new-found confidence to rediscover their roots. Radicals found fresh hope but had not counted on the suffocating legacy of imperialism.

Part of that legacy was the English language and so much that came with it, notably the materialistic value system of the West. To this day, they find their world being squeezed into the Western mould.

Western institutions often dominate their economies. What the West may refer to as modernisation or globalisation they see as Westernisation. Western economies dominate and determine world economies. Either the economies of these Islamic nations buckle under and conform or they are in danger of going under and becoming impoverished. In the 21st century Western imperialism has, to a large extent, shed its military uniform for a pin-striped suit. Governments prepared to go with the flow stand a chance of keeping afloat on the world scene. Any who don't may condemn their people to a life of Third World poverty.

Economic survival has a cost: political, cultural, and religious compromise. To the Islamic purist, it is an attack on the integrity of their religion. Those Islamic leaders who compromise with the West in order to survive are viewed as apostate. Some Muslim countries appear wealthy. Closer examination, however, may reveal that the wealth is largely in the hands of some small ruling dynasty. Those Islamic leaders who appear to have compromised fundamental beliefs in the eyes of radical reformers like Osama bin Laden, under Shariah law, become legitimate targets for Jihad.

The media broadcast Western values to the world. Our soap operas at times portray values that are as unacceptable to Muslims as they ought to be to Christians. The West is accused of exporting pornography and violence. And since the fundamental integration of religion and politics means that religious protest finds political expression, their response to this cultural pollution is often violent. Outgunned by the technological superiority of the West, they are driven to extremes of terrorism and suicide, tragically deceived in resorting to evil to strike out at evil. But, as comes through so strongly in Tolkien's *Lord of the Rings*, evil is true to its nature. It destroys those who would use it to destroy. Hard as it may be for Western minds to understand, Muslims honestly believe that in attacking the West and its influences, they are defending righteousness.

Ajith Fernando, godly leader of Youth for Christ in Sri Lanka, a man with a burden to reach Muslims with the gospel, has said: "Terrorism is the violent response to what the terrorists see as a threat to the freedom and the rights of their people. This perception may be correct or incorrect. The means they use to achieve their ends are certainly wrong, but some of their anger may be justified."

Good people, no matter what religion they follow, are horrified by terrorism. Good, moderate Muslim men and women are no exception. They would want to dissociate themselves totally from such acts. According to their light, many are upright, devout people with a genuine compassion and concern for others. Having lived with a devout Muslim family in a Malay *kampong* (village), I know that they would find it just as painful as we do to see how religion has been abused. Religion does not solve the problem of evil in the human heart. There is only one who can do that for us – our Lord Jesus.[9]

My hours in the darkness of the Coca-Cola factory, huddled alongside a crowd of frightened Muslim men and women, challenged my view of them. The Russian novelist Alexander Solzhenitsyn, lying in a Siberian prison camp, had his presuppositions challenged as he witnessed some appalling and dehumanising horrors. In his book *The Gulag Archipelago*, he wrote:

> It was only when I lay there on rotting prison straw that I sensed within myself the first stirrings of good. Gradually it was disclosed to me that the line separating good and evil passes not through states, nor between classes, nor between political parties either, but right through every human heart, and through all human hearts. This line shifts. Inside us, it oscillates with the years. . . .

Evil is not a problem of communism nor is it the problem of capitalism or Islam – it is my problem. As Paul put it: "All have sinned and fall short of the glory of God."[10] That is a universal truth, for "the heart is deceitful above all things and beyond cure. Who can understand it?"[11] The corruption of the human heart is what lies at the root of the problem. The more we suppress that truth, the more unpredictably it will erupt with devastating results. Evil, left unchecked, will destroy. That is its nature.

At a personal level as well as at the national level our only escape from the hold of evil is to turn from it in repentance. Jesus told us to pray: "Lead us not into temptation, but deliver us from the evil one"[12] – a prayer to turn daily from evil and open ourselves up to God.

When the tower of Siloam fell and innocent people died, Jesus gave us the same message:

> Those eighteen who died when the tower in Siloam fell on them – do you think they were more guilty than all the others living in Jerusalem? I tell you, no! But unless you repent, you too will all perish.[13]

Repentance involves radical surgery. It is both difficult and painful. In Solzhenitsyn's words:

> If only there were evil people out there, insidiously committing evil deeds, and it was only necessary to separate them from the rest of us and destroy them! But the line dividing good and evil cuts through the heart of every human being, and who among us is willing to destroy a piece of their own heart?

Notes

1 Jeremiah 17:9
2 Romans 5:10; John 1:14
3 John 14:6
4 Matthew 1:23
5 John 18:36
6 Matthew 22:21

7 1 Peter 5:8
8 Matthew 7:3
9 Matthew 1:21 cf. Acts 4:12; John 14:6
10 Romans 3:23
11 Jeremiah 17:9
12 Matthew 6:13
13 Luke 13:4–5

CHAPTER SIX

THE GOD WHO SUFFERS

. . . to our wounds only God's wounds can speak.
(Edward Shillito)

Thomas Hamilton was a man with a grudge. He had run boys' clubs, but the local community were suspicious. They banned the clubs, and they were right. His interest in young boys was far from wholesome.

Dunblane, a prosperous commuter town in the central belt of Scotland, was a close-knit community. It was a cold Wednesday morning in March. Fathers had left for work. Mothers had wrapped their children warmly against the cold. The early morning hustle and bustle of breakfast behind them, the children had been bundled off to school. It was just another day. Classes had barely begun when Hamilton strode through the school and joined the children in the gym. It was a place he knew. It was where he had held his boys' clubs.

Mrs Gwenne Mayor had the children of Primary One well organised. They were laughing and playing happily. From

70

under his anorak, Hamilton reached for one of his four pistols. One by one he emptied them, picking off the children as they huddled in a corner around their teacher. In less than three minutes 16 of the infants, and their teacher, lay dead or dying. Then finally, Hamilton turned the gun on himself. Twelve other children lay badly injured, along with the two teachers who had rushed in to help. Our five-year-old niece, Mhairi, was one of those who died.

Emergency teams confronted the scene of carnage. Dead and dying children lay on the floor. John McEwan of the Forth Valley ambulance service described the horror: "It was not so much the dying, it was five-year-old children looking unbelievingly at bullet holes in their arms and legs, and who could not comprehend what was happening . . . the very fact that they were Primary One children meant that words couldn't begin to describe it . . . it was macabre, grotesque and disgusting."

Like any other little girl, Mhairi was a bright and lively five-year-old. But she had a special role in the family. Her father had just died, so she was growing up to be a companion for her mother, Isabel, and three-month-old baby sister, Catherine. Her father, Murray, a lecturer in philosophy in the Department of Religious Studies at Stirling University, had just died at the age of 48. He was not to see the birth of his second child. In a uniquely tragic way his memorial service was to have taken place that very afternoon at Stirling University.

After the memorial service in Dunblane Cathedral, I conducted the service for Mhairi at the same crematorium where, just six months before, I had taken her father's funeral. Immediately after the service, I headed to Heathrow and my flight back to Singapore. Knowing why I had to delay my flight by a day, Singapore Airlines had deferred my ticket.

In normal circumstances I have no trouble sleeping on the overnight flight. I had done it many times before. This time, with great consideration, the airline had allocated three special seats so that I could "stretch out and sleep" for the thirteen-hour journey. Three seats or no three seats, I did not sleep.

As I had boarded the plane, there in the magazine rack was a copy of *Newsweek*. On the cover was a full-page black and white picture of Mhairi staring at me from her class photograph. And all I could think was: WHY? Why the senseless killing of innocents? Why didn't God intervene to stop it all?

In the face of such stark tragedy, many journalists wrote at great length, saying that there are no words to be written. Even to speak of tragedy, one said, is to use a word devalued by overuse. All true. As I sat, I went over and over the funeral service. The reading of Scripture would have brought some comfort, but apart from that, I wondered what else could have been said in the face of such suffering, such agony of loss in a young mother still grieving for her husband. It hurt me – what must she have felt?

How was it vaguely possible for her "to see the present calamity in a true perspective?" We believe that God is good. We believe he is love. We believe that he is sovereign. Then, in the words of Rabbi Harold Kushner: "Why do bad things happen to good people?" If God is love, and God is good and all-powerful, then the existence of evil and our experience of suffering mean we are facing ultimate and unanswerable questions.

Today, in the face of international tensions and rumours of terrorism and war, we are being forced to ask questions that we would rather not have to think about. And when we become victims, marshmallow ideas we may have been fed about God, as if he were some benign eternal Santa Claus, will do little to help us cope with so intense a pain. Ultimately, whatever perspectives bring us a degree of relief, we are going to have to face the truth spelled out in Paul's great doxology:

> Oh, the depth of the riches of the wisdom and knowledge of God! How unsearchable his judgments, and his paths beyond tracing out! Who has known the mind of the Lord? Or who has been his counsellor?[1]

We still look for whatever light we can find. We remind ourselves that God chose to make us the way we are. He knew the limitations we would face. He did not create us to be robots. We are not clones. And when he made us he did not choose to make us immune to suffering. Daringly, he made us in his image. He chose to give us the freedom of choice – with all that the entire gift involved. For with the gift came the freedom to choose good and the freedom to choose evil. He gave us the freedom to obey; the freedom to disobey; the freedom to delight in the law of God; the freedom to walk in the counsel of the ungodly,[2] even the freedom to ignore his very existence and live our own way without any reference to him. Freedom carries consequences. And God knew before he even created the world that it would involve suffering. So when God created us to have the freedom of choice, he did so knowing all the suffering and pain which would arise from our making wrong choices.

The fact that God knew about suffering in his world becomes clearer when we remember that Jesus was active in the creation of our world:

> For by him all things were created: things in heaven and on earth, visible and invisible, whether thrones or powers or rulers or authorities; all things were created by him and for him. He is before all things, and in him all things hold together.[3]

Hard though it may be to fathom, the cross and all that was involved was in the mind of God from the dawn of time. The book of Revelation tells us that the One by whom and for whom all things were created was also "the Lamb that was slain from the creation of the world".[4]

Our salvation was in the mind of God before he ever said, "Let there be light." And he chose us in Christ "before the creation of the world to be holy and blameless in his sight. In love he predestined us to be adopted as his sons through Jesus Christ".[5] So he knew. And he knew at the same time that he would experience suffering more than any of us would ever know.

When God sent his Son into our world he was not wrapped in sanitised cotton wool. He came to a germ-laden cattle trough. While the shepherds on the hills may have enjoyed the angelic choir recital, at street level the singing would soon be replaced with the screams of distraught mothers, agonising for their slaughtered babies. Christ was born into a world of suffering, light-years removed from the sentimentalised images on our Christmas cards.

God is not indifferent. He identifies with our suffering. And he does so without in any way compromising his love or omnipotence. The suffering-love of God binds together two facts of life that are inseparable in our experience: love and suffering. The tension between love and suffering may be beyond the reach of my reason, but that is not to say it is against reason.

Suffering we know. But what do we really mean by love? The word has become debased. It is this that makes it more difficult for us to reconcile suffering with love. Here we can only turn again to the cross – where the justice and wrath of God combines with his love and mercy as he suffers. There at the foot of that cross, while we may not have answers, we are drawn to the only appropriate response – humble worship. For there we see that our God suffers. The only appropriate response I can make is to bow before his cross and say with Job: "My ears had heard of you but now my eyes have seen you. Therefore I despise myself and repent in dust and ashes."[6]

God is no stranger to suffering – he has experienced it for everyone.[7] Bishop James Jones, in his book *Why Do People Suffer?*, tells the poignant story of a school which collapsed in an earthquake:

> A school had caved in, killing all the teachers and most of the children. A little boy, badly maimed, was rescued from the rubble and rushed to hospital. For hours a team of doctors and nurses fought to save his life while his mother waited anxiously outside the operating theatre. After seven hours of painstaking surgery the little boy died.
>
> Instead of leaving it to the nurse to tell the mother, the surgeon went himself. As he broke the dreadful news the mother became hysterical in her grief and attacked the surgeon, pummelling his chest with her fists. But instead of pushing her away, the doctor

held her to himself tightly until the woman's sobbing subsided and she rested cradled in his arms.

And then in the heavy silence the surgeon began to weep. Tears streamed down his face and grief racked his body. For he had come to the hospital the moment he heard that his one and only son had been killed in the same school.

Grief, anger, pain – we experience them all in suffering. And while we may not be able to say so openly, deep down we can even get angry with God. At such a time he will hold us tightly if only we will let him. He, more than anyone, knows just what we are going through. "For God so loved the world that he gave his one and only Son, that whoever believes in him shall not perish but have eternal life."[8]

The godly Archbishop William Temple once observed that people say there cannot be a God of love "because if there was, and he looked upon the world, his heart would break. The church points to the cross and says, 'It did break'".

John Stott, in his book *The Cross of Christ*, strikes a chord that rings true to those of us who have spent a great part of our lives on the foreign mission field. He says:

In the real world of pain, how could one worship a God who was immune to it? I have entered many Buddhist temples in different Asian countries and stood respectfully before the statue of the Buddha, his legs crossed, arms folded, eyes closed, the ghost of a smile playing round his mouth, a remote look on his face, detached from the agonies of the world. But each time, after a while I have had to look away. And in imagination I have turned instead to the lonely, twisted, tortured figure on the cross, nails through hands and feet, back lacerated, limbs wrenched, brow bleeding from thorn pricks, mouth dry and intolerably thirsty, plunged in God-forsaken darkness. That is the God for me! He laid aside His immunity to pain. He entered our world of flesh and blood, tears and death. He suffered for us. Our sufferings become more manageable in the light of His. There is still a question mark against human suffering, but over it we stamp another mark, the cross which symbolizes divine suffering.

In 1983 Eric Wolterstorff, an experienced young climber, fell to his death in a climbing accident in Austria. Eric was in his prime, a young life cut off at 25 years. Eric was deeply loved and mourned by his father Nicholas whose sense of loss was intense. He wrote of his grief in his *Lament For a Son*:

> God is love. That is why he suffers. To love our suffering sinful world is to suffer. God so suffered for the world that he gave up his only Son to suffering. The one who does not see God's suffering does not see his love. God is suffering love. So suffering is down at the centre of things, deep down where the meaning is. Suffering is the meaning of our world. For Love is the meaning. And Love suffers. The tears of God are the meaning of history.

And while that does not answer all our questions, it sheds light into the appalling darkness of suffering. Wolterstorff found he still had a mystery on his hands. He continues:

> But mystery remains: Why isn't Love-*without*-suffering the meaning of things? Why is suffering-Love the meaning? Why does God endure his suffering? Why does he not at once relieve his agony by relieving ours?

To that heart-cry there can be no clinical response. Yet by looking at the cross we find perspective in God's revelation of himself as the God who suffers. Like Job we can only say through the mystery, "My ears had heard of you but now my eyes have seen you."[9] Job did not arrive at a set of neat answers, despite the strenuous efforts of his "expert" counsellors. But in the light of God's self-revelation some of the fog lifted enough for him to do the only thing that he, and any of us, can do – he worshipped.

Reverend Edward Shillito ministered at a church just outside London early in the last century. He was moved by the appalling sufferings of those whose bodies were grotesquely maimed and disfigured in the battles of the First World War. As he visited and saw their suffering he grappled with issues of faith. His struggles were poured out in the many poems he wrote. One that has been frequently quoted is addressed to the "Jesus of the Scars" – the crucified, suffering Christ who showed his wounds to his disciples. It ends with these moving words:

> . . . Lord Jesus, by Thy Scars we claim Thy grace.
>
> If when the doors are shut, Thou drawest near,
>   Only reveal those hands, that side of Thine;
> We know to-day what wounds are, have no fear,
>   Show us Thy Scars, we know the countersign.
>
> The other gods were strong; but Thou wast weak;
>   They rode, but Thou didst stumble to a throne;
> But to our wounds only God's wounds can speak,
>   And not a god has wounds, but Thou alone.

To the mocking question "Where is your God?" when we face pain beyond expression, we do not have all the answers. But we have a God with wounds.

Notes

1 Romans 11:33–34
2 Psalm 1
3 Colossians 1:16–17
4 Revelation 13:8
5 Ephesians 1:4–5
6 Job 42:5–6
7 Hebrews 2:9
8 John 3:16
9 Job 42:5

CHAPTER SEVEN

THE FEAR OF MEANINGLESSNESS

Providence is a Christian's diary, but not his Bible.
(Thomas Watson)

There can be few more numbing experiences than having to work on an assembly line in a car factory, keeping pace with a moving belt, condemned to repeat the same operation over and over again. I know. I've tried it. While studying engineering as a student apprentice by courtesy of the Ford Motor Company, some of us had the unique experience when our college had its summer vacation of being allowed to do practical studies in production engineering methods in the factory at Dagenham.

On one occasion during my vacation, I asked for, and was granted, permission to work on an assembly line for a week. For 40 hours, over five days, I lifted a never-ending succession of flywheel bell housings and put them onto a row of slowly moving gearboxes. With the help of an overhead power tool which I would pull down to each new box, I fastened the bolts holding the two parts together – again and again and again.

My back ached; my legs grew tired; my brain died! I have never known time to pass so slowly. The arrival of the tea trolley ladies was a major event: ten minutes to sit on the floor, my back against a bin full of gearboxes, and read the newspaper. The half-hour lunch break in the canteen was the only ray of sun in the drabness of the day. And when the time came to clock off it would have taken more than a herd of wild horses to stop me from getting to the front of the mob, in the rush to burst through the factory gates to freedom. It was a week when life seemed to have lost all meaning and purpose. I have great sympathy for those millions around the world who earn their bread and butter on an assembly line and have to pass such a large amount of time with little more purpose to such a large part of their lives.

My original employer is credited with having invented or at least developed the whole concept of mass production around an assembly line. Whether or not it was the sheer monotonous emptiness of life on the assembly line that prompted Henry J. Ford to say that "history is bunk", I could not say. Somehow I doubt whether he spent any of his time tied to the line. But I could be wrong. At least he produced a sound bite that has cheered the heart of many a schoolchild! What he actually said, however, was more profound and penetrating. The *Chicago Tribune* in 1916 actually reported him as saying: "History is more or less bunk. It's tradition. We don't want tradition. We want to live in the present. And the only history that is worth a tinker's damn is the history we make."

History and the Classics may not have been Henry Ford's strong point. But as an industrialist and a manufacturer of cars he was no fool. He had an objective – to create a car for the masses. To that end he experimented, rationalising different procedures to speed up construction and reduce costs. It was his efforts to achieve his goal that led to the mass production techniques of the assembly line. Model Ts rolled off in their millions. His vision was realised. Manufacturing was revolutionised, factory workers dehumanised. He broke the mould. He "made history". And at the end of the day it was worth more than a "tinker's damn" to his shareholders.

History, far from being "more or less bunk", has significance. All of us are a part of history. In it we find meaning. The fact that we live means that we "make history". It gives us significance and meaning. The wise will discover the particular significance life has for them and the significance they can give to history. To feel that my life has no meaning and that history has no purpose is soul-destroying.

Macbeth's lines on receiving news of his wife's suicide could have come from any factory worker on an assembly line. Only in his case, it was the murderous ambition and guilt of Lady Macbeth, together with his evil deeds, that brought this dark pessimism of meaninglessness:

> To-morrow, and to-morrow, and to-morrow,
> Creeps in this petty pace from day to day
> To the last syllable of recorded time,
> And all our yesterdays have lighted fools
> The way to dusty death.

For him, history was not "more or less bunk" – everything had become meaningless. It had no more meaning other than lighting "fools the way to dusty death". There are echoes here from the book of Ecclesiastes, where a life lived without God is so accurately described as "utterly meaningless . . . There is no remembrance of men of old, and even those who are yet to come will not be remembered by those who follow".[1] He calls life nothing but "a chasing after the wind".

With poetic, but deadly logic Macbeth goes on:

> Out, out, brief candle!
> Life's but a walking shadow, a poor player
> That struts and frets his hour upon the stage
> And then is heard no more: it is a tale
> Told by an idiot, full of sound and fury, signifying nothing.

A fear that our life has no real meaning or purpose, no more significance than a candle, is not uncommon. If, in fact, I am nothing more than a by-product of some inanimate bang; if I only exist thanks to a random aberration in some primordial soup kitchen, then the reality of the evil I see on all sides brings me nothing but intimations of dread.

If in my worldview there is no place for God, then the logic is frightening. If a righteous, loving God does not exist, what is good and what is evil? Is there any difference or is it all in the mind? And if I sense a fear of evil, where am I to go for protection?

As Sartre put it in his book *Existentialism and Human Emotions*: "Dostoyevsky said, 'If God didn't exist, everything would be possible. . . .' Indeed, everything is permissible if God does not exist, and as a result man is forlorn, because neither within him nor without does he find anything to cling to." A world without God would bring us to the same conclusion as the Spock of *Star Trek* fame – "There's life, Jim, but not as we know it." A world without God would be hell – ultimate separation from God.

But we don't live in such a world. This is not hell. God has not removed himself from his world. Life is not meaningless. We live in time surrounded by the infinity of space and that inescapable sense that there is an ultimate power. As H. G. Wells said with some perception in his unusual book *God the Invisible King*:

> And those whose acquiescence in the idea of God is merely intellectual are in no better case than those who deny God altogether. They may have all the forms of truth and not divinity. The religion of the atheist with a God-shaped blank at its heart and the persuasion of the unconverted theologian, are both like lamps unlit. The lit lamp has no difference in form from the lamp unlit. But the lit lamp is alive and the lamp unlit is asleep or dead.

That "God-shaped blank" is in the heart of each of us. Only God can fill the void. Augustine wrote in his *Confessions*: "You stimulate [us] to take pleasure in praising you, because you have made us for yourself, and our hearts are restless until they can find peace in you."

Religion is our human initiative to try and fill that blank space. As Christians we believe it was God, not we ourselves, who took the initiative to fill that blank. It is his nature to communicate. And the God above us became the God among us – Immanuel. John MacArthur, in his book *How to Get the Most from God's Word*, has expressed it this way:

> All mankind is trapped on planet Earth, captive to time and space and surrounded by an endless universe. Many sense in the deepest parts of their beings that there is an ultimate power or God. And so they try to discover how they can know this Supreme Being. The result is religion, the invention of man in his attempt to find God.

Christianity, however, teaches that we don't find God, because God has already found us. He has disclosed Himself to us through His Word. In the Old and New Testaments of Holy Scripture we have the unveiling of God.

The Bible bridges the entire history of the earth. During those long centuries God was always disclosing Himself, because it is in His nature to communicate. An artist paints and a singer sings because the ability is in them. God speaks because He desires to make Himself known to His creatures. Francis Schaeffer, referring to God, wrote, "He is there, and He is not silent."

God's revelation of himself presents us with an understanding of world history from eternity to eternity. It is revolutionary. It tells us that God is not detached from his world. "In the beginning God created the heavens and the earth."[2] God did not then shoot off to some remote galaxy and hide away. He continues to sustain his creation "by his powerful word".[3]

He is the Sovereign Lord.[4] History is not more or less bunk; it is something in which God is intimately involved. Under his mighty hand, history has a destiny. It is going somewhere. And since each one of us is a part of developing history, every life has significance and meaning.

Scripture is not in the business of spelling out the specifics of exactly what will happen ten years down the line. Time and space are too vast for one volume to detail all that could happen. Scripture, however, pulls back the curtains to let us see the forces that are at work controlling and shaping the world's destiny. And that is where we must look if we want to find "a true perspective" when facing the enigma of evil in our world.

What we do discover is that, whatever evil may happen in this world, ultimately God will overrule it for his purposes.

We are to trust him even when what he allows seems contradictory. The cross is a supreme example of how God overruled evil for his glory. At times he may make use of strange forces to either protect or correct us, as Habakkuk was to learn,[5] and that must deepen our trust in him even when we do not understand. In the words of F. W. Faber's hymn:

> Thrice blest is he to whom is given
> The instinct that can tell
> That God is on the field when he
> Is most invisible.

Thomas Watson in *A Body of Divinity* expresses it quaintly:

Indeed as Augustine says well, "We are beholden to wicked men, who against their wills do us good." As the corn is beholden to the flail to thresh off its husks, or as the iron is beholden to the file to brighten it, so the godly are beholden to the wicked, though it be against their will, to brighten and refine their graces.

God in his wisdom permits evil – all history proves that to us. He allows people and nations to walk in their own ways[6] but that does not mean he has any hand in their evil. He cannot act contrary to his nature. Some things we may not understand. What is clear is that he will somehow bring good out of it all.

He is the Lord of history. We witness his dealings with nations. Sometimes we see that evil is apparently allowed to flourish unchecked. It even appears to enjoy success. Sometimes we are tempted to envy the wicked. Like the psalmists in Psalm 37 and 73 we wonder why it is that some people, who live without any reference to God in their lives, seem to

THE FEAR OF MEANINGLESSNESS

prosper. Psalm 37 encourages us not to let their seeming success undermine our trust in God, while the 73rd psalm reminds us of their final destiny.[7] In faith we recognise the providences of God but at the same time we do not equate the evidences of success as proof positive of God's blessing.

In our personal lives, the words of the Puritan Thomas Watson are well worth applying: "Providence is a Christian's diary, but not his Bible." This is an important principle to bear in mind when we tell others of the Lord's particular dealings with us. As Eric Alexander has said: "Christian experience is not the same thing as the experience of some Christians." God's word, not my experiences of life, is where I find true meaning.

The preacher in Ecclesiastes, who experienced the fear of meaninglessness, gives the antidote to it when he says: "Here is the conclusion of the matter: fear God and keep his commandments, for this is the whole duty of man."[8]

Notes

1 Ecclesiastes 1:2, 11
2 Genesis 1:1
3 Hebrews 1:3
4 Acts 4:24
5 Habakkuk 1:12
6 Acts 14:16
7 Psalm 73:3, 16–20
8 Ecclesiastes 12:13

CHAPTER EIGHT

MAKING SENSE OF OUR TROUBLED WORLD

Why do the nations rage? (Psalm 2:1)

Why did the apostles turn to the second psalm (Acts 4:23ff.) for help when the Sanhedrin was out for their blood? The answer surely is that those scriptures that spoke of God as their Sovereign Lord were the assurance they needed that their destiny was in his hands alone.

As a child, I remember seeing vast wall charts covered with strange-looking beasts all over them, an artist's impression from the book of Revelation. The charts, so we were to understand, spelt out in detail God's plan for the end times. Master the chart and you knew exactly what to expect – more or less. Those who preached from their charts seemed to be pulling rabbits out of hats – something that should have put me on my guard. As a boy of ten I was overawed.

As the years have gone by, I have not been able to find any of these "rabbits" in Scripture. What I do see is that Jesus will return to this world in great triumph. He will bring everything to a glorious consummation. He warned that there would be "wars and rumours of wars" in "the last days" – that time between his first and second coming – and told us to be ready when he does come. All that is crystal clear.

With 24/7 news coverage we have more than just "rumours of wars" – the wars are played out before our eyes. There would appear to be an escalation of violence in our world and it seems to parallel the cyclic intensification of evil portrayed in Revelation. This is all, perhaps, an indicator that our Lord's return may not be long delayed.

What the second psalm gives us is an overarching perspective on what is going on in our world. "Now pay attention," as the advertisement says, "here comes the technical bit." We will need to read the psalm.

It may make things clearer, as we read, to think of it as starting off with a prologue by a commentator or chorus, as Shakespeare would have called it. Today it would be the role of the TV commentator or a political affairs editor. The chorus introduces us to world governments and politicians, and their reaction to any suggestion that they ought to submit to God's rule and authority. The commentator then comments on their actions and reactions.

After that, the scene shifts from earth and we eavesdrop on a dialogue between the Lord God and his Anointed One. This has been stimulated by the politicians' rebellious attitude to God's rule and authority. We may have first-hand evidence on our TV screens as to what world leaders at the United Nations are saying in the Security Council, but here in this psalm we glimpse the unseen council in heaven. There we learn of the authority the Lord God has given to his Anointed One – his Son. And after being privy to that scene, our reporter returns to challenge us with the implications this has for us in our world.

PSALM 2

The commentator

The issue of a global rebellion

> [1] Why do the nations conspire ("rage" – margin)
> and the peoples plot in vain?
> [2] The kings of the earth take their stand
> and the rulers gather together
> against the LORD
> and against his Anointed One.

The conspiracy of world rulers

> [3] "Let us break their chains," they say,
> "and throw off their fetters."

God's response

God's assessment of their rebellion

> [4] The One enthroned in heaven laughs;
> the Lord scoffs at them.
> [5] Then he rebukes them in his anger
> and terrifies them in his wrath, saying,

God's action

> [6] "I have installed my King
> on Zion, my holy hill."

God's commission

> [7] I will proclaim the decree of the LORD:
> He said to me, "You are my Son;
> today I have become your Father.

God's promise

> [8] Ask of me,
>   and I will make the nations your inheritance,
>   the ends of the earth your possession.
> [9] You will rule them with an iron sceptre;
>   you will dash them to pieces like pottery."

The commentator

The warning and appeal to all rebels

> [10] Therefore, you kings, be wise;
>   be warned, you rulers of the earth.
> [11] Serve the LORD with fear
>   and rejoice with trembling.
> [12] Kiss the Son, lest he be angry
>   and you be destroyed in your way,
>   for his wrath can flare up in a moment.
>   Blessed are all who take refuge in him.

Now it could help our understanding to know where this psalm came from. Clearly, it is connected with some historical event of considerable significance – a royal coronation at a time of rebellion. But just whose coronation was it? And what rebellion is it talking about?

The simple answer to both questions is: we simply don't know. Perhaps, if we did, we might feel it was limited to that event alone. However, the way in which the New Testament writers return again and again to this psalm indicates that to them it had an application that went beyond any specific event.

According to the apostles,[1] this psalm was written by David. Clearly, it moves on beyond David and through the royal dynasty of the house of David – a psalm fitting for the coronation of all the kings of Israel and Judah. Its underlying premise applies to all wise rulers: submission to God, the ultimate authority and ruler of all.

The imagery of war and rebellion may have come from David's first-hand experience. But clearly, from the way the Jews, along with New Testament writers, viewed the psalm, it pointed directly to great David's greater Son – the coming Messiah.

The six-pointed Star of David on Israel's flag serves as a reminder of the great significance of the Davidic dynasty. The origins of that star are shrouded in mystery but it has become the most common and universally recognised sign of Jewish identity and embodies their messianic hope. That hope is based on the golden age when David was the greatest warrior-king Israel had ever known. The kings who followed David were a disappointment. Only the Messiah King, "great David's greater son", could fulfil all that the psalm foretold. The final destiny to which the psalm points is the final victory of the Lord God and his Messiah – and that is the clear message that heaven takes up in the book of Revelation when it sings: "The kingdom of the world has become the kingdom of our Lord and of his Christ, and he will reign for ever and ever."[2]

The king referred to in the psalm is called the Lord's "Anointed One". That word "anointed" is the word "Messiah" in the Hebrew, or "Christ" in the Greek. The psalmist shows us how the Lord's "Anointed One" is appointed as God's Viceroy on earth. As Lord of the earth he is the One to whom the nations are to give their allegiance.

In one sense, every king of Israel anointed by a prophet was an "anointed one" – "a messiah". If he was a true "defender of the faith" of Israel and lived in submission to God, then his rule carried divine authority. As God's chosen servant and representative on earth he would enjoy God's protection and authority in the execution of his office. The fact of history, however, was that most of Israel's kings failed miserably on all counts. They did not live up to the ideal.

It is only in Jesus that the psalm finds fulfilment. The royal families of Israel and Judah were, for the most part, a disgrace. Understandably, their subjects lost respect for them as they failed in their duties as leaders.

The dialogue behind the psalm is significant. It is between the Lord God and his Anointed One. As the psalm unfolds, it alternates between this world of time and space, and the timeless councils of eternity. Another way to understand it is to think of it as having four sections:

1. The world about us (verses 1–3)

We begin the psalm with a look around us.

First voice – the commentator

He starts where we are – on earth and facing troubles. He looks at the state of the world about him, much as we have been doing in these preceding chapters and he cries out, "Why do the nations rage?"[3]

Second voice – the politicians

Part of the answer to his question comes as he listens in on the councils and deliberations of world leaders. They brazenly declare their independence from the Almighty and, specifically, want to break from any ties that would bind them to God and his Anointed One. "Let us free ourselves from their rule," they say. "Let us throw off their control."[4]

2. The God above us (verses 4–6)

The scene then shifts to a secret dialogue which starts in heaven – the principal characters being the Lord and his Son, the Messiah.

Speaker – the Lord God
The Lord God is first to speak. He laughs derisively over the futility of the politicians' rebellion and all their efforts to run affairs of state without him. His laughter is not amusement. It is a sense of incredulity that politicians and presidents should think they could succeed in running his world without any intention of submitting to him as its Creator.

But it is no laughing matter – it makes him angry. And in righteous anger he declares that despite the rulers' desire to go it alone, he installs his King Messiah on Zion, his holy hill. And while this world takes steps to put an end to the rule of his Christ, God treats that with the derision it deserves.

3. The God among us (verses 7–9)

With mention of Zion we return once again to earth – for the God above us is Immanuel – the God among us.

It is then that we hear the Son speaking.

Speaker – the Son
He refers to "the decree of the Lord". In that decree God has instructed him to ask to be given the nations and ends

of the earth as an inheritance, and the authority to rule over them with a rod of iron.

That rule of Christ is seen as a fait accompli by heaven, but it is something which has still to be worked out on earth. And it is to the New Testament that we turn to see how it is accomplished. From there, we learn that Jesus began this rule when he rose from the dead and ascended to heaven to sit down at the right hand of God,[5] "from whence he will come to judge the living and the dead".

4. The mission before us (verses 10–12)

Now our commentator brings us the challenge. He brings us down to earth with a bump. The application of all that has been revealed is to be taken seriously as we face our world.

Speaker – the commentator
Then comes an appeal to the powers that be – the kings, rulers, politicians, presidents, and governments – that they be wise. They will never thwart God's ultimate purpose to install his Messiah King. They will never ultimately prevent his rule from extending over all the earth. Those who come under his rule will find him to be a source of blessing and a refuge. Those who resist will find nothing, but will be left to face his wrath – and discover that "it is a dreadful thing to fall into the hands of the living God".[6]

Their only hope is to bow before the Lord God and his Christ and offer their loyalty. Failure to comply will bring wrath. It is only faith and trust in Christ that will bring refuge and happiness (10–12).

96 NOTHING ELSE TO FEAR

A clearer mandate for world mission could not be found anywhere, for all authority from the Lord God has been given to the Lord's "Anointed One".

As we listen to our Lord's last words to his disciples we find echoes of this psalm when he says:

> I have been given all authority in heaven and on earth. Go, then, to all peoples everywhere and make them my disciples: baptize them in the name of the Father, the Son, and the Holy Spirit, and teach them to obey everything I have commanded you. And I will be with you always, to the end of the age.[7]

Here in this psalm we are given a broad perspective on our world of time from a viewpoint that is timeless. It is a glimpse behind the scenes. Clearly, the psalm does not end with a mushy multi-faith appeal for us to go into all the world and preach comfortable spirituality. It is the uniqueness of the Anointed One, Christ, that comes through loud and clear – the unequivocal message that all men and women everywhere must submit to him or experience God's wrath.

The clear point at issue here is that apart from Christ, we have nothing to offer this world. He is the unique revelation of God to our world. "In the past God spoke to our forefathers through the prophets and in various ways, but in these last days he has spoken to us by his Son."[8]

Fear may drive us to make compromising statements about what we believe. Of course, all people everywhere have a right to choose what they wish to believe. But that freedom of choice in no way compromises our conviction that salvation is to be found in Christ alone.[9] The Bible is never vague on that issue.

Vagueness is the current vogue when it comes to matters of faith, but such vagueness cannot alter God's truth. Writing to his congregation in Glasgow, Dr Sinclair Ferguson says:

> To speak of him as God incarnate, the only Saviour, as humanity's only hope in modern pluralistic Britain, is no longer socially tolerated and certainly not politically correct.
>
> Orthodox Christian witness now stands condemned by the worst of all pejorative modern terms: "fundamentalism".
>
> We have been called to be Christ's witnesses in this society. Most of us daily experience that same pressure to dumb-down Christian witness in the office or hospital, in our places of recreation, in the neighbourhood and perhaps even in the family. It is not easy to be Christ's in modern Britain. . . .
>
> A positive way to look at it is this: we are called to serve Christ today in a context just like that of the first Christians – one in which Jesus was tolerated so long as no one made exclusive claims for him; OK to say "Jesus is my Lord"; not OK to say "Jesus is *the* Lord".

Notes

1 Acts 4:25
2 Revelation 11:15
3 Psalm 2:1
4 Psalm 2:3 (*Today's English Version*)
5 Matthew 28:18; Ephesians 1:20–23; 1 Peter 3:22; Revelation 1:5; 2:26–27
6 Hebrews 10:31
7 Matthew 28:18–20 (*Today's English Version*)
8 Hebrews 1:1–2
9 Acts 4:12

CHAPTER NINE

THE HEART OF THE PROBLEM

The state of our world today is one of organised insanity. (Dr Martyn Lloyd-Jones)

The gentle, pink warmth of the cherry blossom-lined avenues along the waterfront was in stark contrast to the harsh reality of everything that was going on in the UN building behind us. There, in a maze of corridors, offices and conference rooms, solemn dignitaries walked purposefully about their business. Politicians and diplomats in dark suits stood huddled in earnest discussion, relieved by the occasional splash of bright colour – an African delegate in national dress. Hustle and bustle was on every side. And, weaving our way through it all we walked, crocodile fashion, like an expectant group of school children following their teacher.

Our "teacher", Natasha, hardly fitted the stereotype. She was stylishly petite and smart, a young woman from Belarus who looked for all the world as if she had just sprung from the parallel bars of some Olympic gymnasium. Dressed in an impeccable two-piece suit, she spoke perfect English with just the merest trace of an accent to betray her roots. Her grasp of all that was going on was impressive. She was politically astute.

As we approached the first conference room our way was barred.

"They're in session. Can't go in. Major decisions. Shaping history!" Her solemn tone was conspiratorial.

And there was something sobering about the fact that all that separated us from the "major decisions" that were "shaping history" was the thickness of a wooden door. Behind it, a small group of men and women were locked in conference, grappling with issues that affected the fate of thousands. It called for reflection.

Just a few minutes before, we had been in a different world, the mayhem that is Grand Central Station. Entertained, we had watched the crowds rushing madly about their business through New York's sculptured marble cathedral of art deco. We waited and watched to see whether any of the Hollywood greats would appear. They didn't – or if they did we missed them. Cary Grant running to board his train to Chicago was conspicuous by his absence. So, not too surprised, we set off down 42nd Street to the eastern waterfront. In a few hundred yards, the rush of the city was forgotten. We were inside the United Nations complex, an island – a secular "Vatican" – in the heart of "the world's capital".

But it wasn't just the cherry blossom outside that clashed with the reality within. It was what our guide did not say that made me think. Living and working with the Javanese for over 20 years taught me to listen for what is *not* said. The Javanese, in their refined politeness, have developed beating about the bush into an art form. To grasp what they may really be saying you have to learn the art of sifting words. It is important to discover what has been left unsaid. Often it was silence on an issue that spoke volumes. Natasha did not beat about the bush in her commentary on the UN. She did not consciously omit anything as far as we could see. But I was reacting to what she had left unsaid. Did she really believe that it was the deliberations of the people in this building that shaped history?

For me, that was a statement too far. Today's events become tomorrow's history. But far from shaping our history, more often than not history has an unfathomable dynamic of its own. Presidents and politicians grapple with issues on a global scale but the deep cross-currents of competing human value systems ultimately defy any human ability to direct, let alone control, the outcome. Listening to some of the debates that take place in the UN, it is hard not to feel that forces are at work which are beyond our human ability to control. No wonder the psalmist asks, "Why do the nations rage?"

The phrase is evocative of violent mobs of angry rioters rampaging in mass demonstrations. One commentator paraphrases the verse as "Why is the great tumult of nations mustering for war?" Much of our news coverage on TV shows us more of this kind of thing than we care to watch: world superpowers marshalling their troops for war; mobs venting their anger; anti-globalisation demonstrators wantonly destroying property; wild fundamentalist extremists shooting off their Kalashnikovs into the air.

The word indicating the uproar in the first verse of Psalm 2 is translated differently in various translations. That is because the word means more than just uproar. It carries a sinister implication captured by the translators of the *New*

International Version to indicate that it is not a mere storm in a teacup. The rage is evidence of a disturbing conspiracy – "Why do the nations conspire and the peoples plot in vain?"[1]

To "conspire"[2] is to do something against the law, to commit an unlawful action agreed in secret – a scheme to co-operate towards a common end. And that is what the nations are pictured as doing in their angry conspiracy against God. Such a "conspiracy theory" behind all the turmoil we see in the nations raises questions. What is it about? And who is behind it all?

The question "What is it all about?" finds immediate answer in the text. The conspiracy is all about rejecting the rule and authority of God. And specifically, here it is portrayed as involving those who represent us – our kings and rulers. "The kings of the earth take their stand and the rulers gather together against the Lord and against his Anointed One." "Let us break their chains," they say, "and throw off their fetters",[3] as if they were sitting like some UN council deliberating on world issues and, in particular, the right of the Lord and his Christ to rule over them.

The nations: "The peoples and nations, as if in a tumultuous assembly, raging with a fury like the raging of the sea, designing to resist God's government" is how the *Jamieson-Fausset-Brown Bible Commentary* paraphrases the verse. Matthew Henry in his commentary writes: "They rage and fret; they gnash their teeth for vexation at the setting up of Christ's kingdom; it creates in them the utmost uneasiness, and fills them with indignation." In other words, the conspiracy has a focus. That focus is the rule of God. The conspiracy is therefore a concerted opposition to the establishment of Christ's kingdom on earth.

And that of course anticipates an answer as to who is behind it. Basically, the struggle is between heaven and hell. Satan is "the prince of the power of the very air we breathe in and the god of the world we live in" (Matthew Henry) and his kingdom is well established. When the kingdom of God gains, he loses. Martin Luther's well-known hymn reassures us: "His doom is writ; A word shall quickly slay him." But that does not mean that Satan is about to give up without a struggle of cosmic proportions.

When Jesus came into our world, "a second Adam to the fight and to the rescue came". And his coming was a declaration of war. The powers of evil went into high gear and the evidence for that is found throughout the gospels. The words with which Jesus opened his ministry, "Repent for the kingdom of heaven is near", threw down the gauntlet to those powers of evil. And when he taught his followers to pray, "Your kingdom come, your will be done, on earth as it is in heaven" he was teaching us a principle of life that would inevitably mean a confrontation with a world that has signed up to the silent conspiracy and says, "Let us free ourselves from their rule . . . let us throw off their control."[4]

From its opening verse we see how this psalm was viewed by New Testament writers as a key to understanding the world around them. It took them to the core issue: one planet with two worlds living side by side. One world prays, "Our Father in heaven . . . your kingdom come, your will be done, on earth as it is in heaven." The other world turns its back on heaven, saying, "Let us free ourselves from their rule."

Such diametrically opposite views on the authority of God will inevitably mean that those who are serious about following Jesus will be out of step with the world. The world is united in its stand "against the Lord and against his Anointed One". This, surely, is why Jesus warned us that following him involves a cross. "In this world you will have trouble"[5] – we'd better believe it!

I watched with admiration on one occasion as the British foreign secretary delivered a speech at the United Nations in New York one day, only to fly back home across the Atlantic to escort some of the UN officials around the corridors of 10 Downing Street the very next day. One wonders at the dedication of these men and women burning themselves out as they jet-set between the world's capitals in their never-ending round of diplomatic endeavour to find the answer to the question, "Why do the nations rage?"

What this second psalm shows us however is that they, like all of us, are involved, whether consciously or not, in this silent conspiracy. We live in a world which rejects the rule and authority of God. Tragically, that is not something they are likely to factor into their deliberations at the UN! They, like the vast majority of all those whom they represent, do not treat the Maker's handbook seriously.

Some things our governments legislate for fly in the face of God's word, ranging from issues of abortion, gay rights, environmental pollution, to the tragic indifference shown in addressing some of the appalling situations that exist in Third World countries. These are the tip of the iceberg against which the *Titanic* of our once Christian culture is foundering.

Of course we recognise that many decent men and women are honourable and serious, and work earnestly for those things that are right and just within the parameters of their ideological framework. But righteousness exalts a nation and when God's revelation of that righteousness is ignored, we are in a parlous state.

We live in a "three-minute culture". Thanks to the media and our seeming inability to concentrate for more than a few minutes, few people have the patience to sit and listen to reasoned arguments. We live on sound bites. But as the song by Don Schlitz and Paul Overstreet puts it: "Try as I may I could never explain what I hear when you don't say a thing . . . You say it best when you say nothing at all." And it is the sound bites we never hear from our leaders that give the clue. There is silence on issues where God speaks, evidence of complicity in the silent conspiracy that says: "Let us break their chains . . . and throw off their fetters."[6] "Let us free ourselves from their rule . . . let us throw off their control."[7]

The "chains and fetters" referred to in the psalm are words taken from the world of agriculture – the bridle, bit and reins – all of them designed for the control and well-being of the animal and its rider. Seen in that light, the conspiracy of the nations to "break their chains . . . and throw off their fetters" is the height of madness.

When driving through the rice fields along the pot-holed roads in Java, it was not unusual to come suddenly upon on a slow, lumbering cart being drawn by a couple of weary-looking water buffalo. On a good day, these carts probably reach a maximum speed of around two miles an hour. From time to time you would find one parked at the roadside, its driver scooping water from a nearby ditch to throw over the beasts to cool them down. They, poor animals, lived for the time when they could be unhitched and led off into some muddy pool for a final cool-off at the end of the day. Such an ox cart lumbering in your path as you rounded a corner at speed could be unnerving.

But just as long as the driver wasn't asleep, and the yoke and reins were in place, all was well. The animals would continue on a predictably straight course. No peasant in his right mind would dream of taking his unwieldy cart onto the highway without the yoke and reins firmly in place. With the shimmering heat-haze rising from the tarmac, and cars screaming past at speeds only a fatalist would attempt, it was the one thing that ensured safety for all concerned. Only a madman would throw away the reins.

While I was still at high school, I spent Saturday mornings earning pocket money as a "grease monkey", servicing cars. I developed a lifelong love for cars. As an engineering student, I built my first "special" based on an Austin Seven. I spent a great deal of time modifying the old beam axle at the front. It was cut in half, and converted into a simple form of independent suspension. That was relatively easy. The difficult part came trying to modify the steering linkage. That took time and effort. The connection between the steering wheel and road needed to be more than just wishful thinking! What kind of fool would I have been if I had said, "The new suspension is so smooth – I won't bother about the brakes and steering"? No engineer worth his salt would say, "Let's ignore the steering, throw away the track rods and forget the ball joints." But that is the level of our rebellion against God.

As a mission director in the UK, one of my more pleasant tasks was the opportunity to visit with our missionaries in East Asia. On one visit to Japan, Adèle and I were sent off on our own to the south of the northern island of Hokkaido. We were going to visit Chefoo, one of our mission schools. Not knowing a word of Japanese, and being totally mystified by the Japanese script, we were concerned to know where to get off the train.

"Oh, you just get off at 19 minutes past four," our hostess informed us.

"But supposing the train is late?" we asked.

"It won't be – unless there's an earthquake," came the confident reply.

Before we could find out what we should do if there was an earthquake, the train had set off down the platform. At 4:19 p.m. precisely, we drew into our station and were met by a reception committee of excited children. This was Japan. We would never dare to predict a train's arrival so accurately in the UK.

Ask any British railway commuter and you will get a very different story. We don't need anything as outlandish as an earthquake to make our trains late. Leaves on the line, powdered snow, vandalism, failure of the driver to show up, track repairs, fog . . . our rail services can come up with the most bizarre list of excuses. They may work hard to try and overcome the problems and improve the service. But as far as I know no one has yet suggested: "Let's tear up the tracks and throw away the signals."

Yet here, in a nutshell, is the madness of our 21st century rebellion. We have thrown away those guiding rails the Creator has laid down in his handbook. With 1000 cubic centimetres of grey matter and a few neurons between our ears, we dare to believe that we can run our lives and our world without reference to the Creator. We have exchanged the law of God for licence. If it seems right or feels good then go for it. Everyone does what is right in their own eyes. Is it any wonder there is so much fear and uncertainty?

The sum of our rulers' combined wisdom is to ignore God. And the language of the psalm indicates that this, far from being a passive omission, is aggressive opposition to the kingdom of God – that kingdom of men and women who live in the "obedience that comes from faith".[8] The nations fail to recognise the recklessness of ignoring those guidelines that God has set out for us in his word for our own good.

What with communist uprisings and then militant Islamic extremists, we have had more experiences of riots in Java than we care to think about. When mobs rampaged through the streets of Jakarta, reason was abandoned. It was blind chaos, mayhem. The rule of law meant nothing. Shops were looted and burned. Cars were overturned. People were shot, clubbed, knifed. It was terrifying to witness.

When mobs run amok, law and order break down. Panic reaches fever pitch. Reason is thrown to the winds. The law of the jungle takes over. And then suddenly, as if someone has pulled a switch, the mobs slowly melt away into the back streets and an eerie calm takes over. Apart from an odd individual picking his way through the debris, the streets are empty. The atmosphere is electric. You look nervously in all directions. You feel naked and vulnerable.

It is not until you see, through the smoking wreckage littered across the road, the forces of law and order in their armoured cars, that a sense of security is restored. Troops station themselves at intervals on either side of the road. Slowly, normality returns and the tension eases. People reappear and walk down to what is left of the shops. Little by little, life returns to normal. And you realise that the bit and bridle supplied by the law, far from being a strait jacket, is a life jacket. Just so, God's word was not given to destroy liberty but to make us truly free. Jesus said, "I am come that they might have life, and that they might have it more abundantly."[9]

Frequently, we watch statesmen log countless hours in their attempts to solve world crises. The frightening awareness of the destructive power of evil drives all of us to seek solutions. Yet tragically, the cycle of violence is not broken. We watch nations and world movements set against one another. Any who do not feel a sense of dismay and fear are, in Mrs Beaver's words, either "braver than most or else just silly". The clear evidence of what happens when a world tries to live without God is all about us.

Shortly before he passed away, Dr Martyn Lloyd-Jones preached from this second psalm at a gathering in Glasgow. He spoke of international tensions of the time, and while evil has been with us from the beginning of history, his statement then that "the state of our world today is one of organised insanity" seems very relevant.

The psalmist's opening "Why?" may not have been a question so much as an expression of incredulity. How can we be so foolish as to think that we can live as God intended us to live without reference to the guidelines he laid down for us in his word? To live without God is to live "imagining a vain thing". The silent conspiracy of our world will not succeed. God will have his way. The wonder is that in order for that to come about, he so loved this rebellious world that he sent his only Son so that all who will accept him as their Lord will discover his love and mercy. And the psalm indicates there is more to say about that.

Notes

1 Psalm 2:1
2 The Hebrew word *ragash* signifies uproar, turmoil and rage

– the preferred choice of some translations – but *ragash* is rage with a dark side – conspiracy.

3 Psalm 2:1–3
4 Psalm 2:3 (*Today's English Version*)
5 John 16:33
6 Psalm 2:1–3
7 Psalm 2:3 (*Today's English Version*)
8 Romans 1:5
9 John 10:10 (*King James Version*)

CHAPTER TEN

THE HEART OF HISTORY

. . . a guilty world is washed by love's pure stream.
(Graham Kendrick)

As we read on into the next section of the second psalm, we find something that on the surface seems disturbing. The psalm looks away from the state of rebellion in the world around us to the God who is enthroned above us. And we find him laughing. That is worrying.

The fear of the Lord is one thing, but does God mock us in all our troubles? An angry God enthroned who laughs, scoffs, rebukes and terrifies seems to be at variance with all we know of his love and mercy and gracious forgiveness. The passage states:

The One enthroned in heaven laughs; the Lord scoffs at them. Then he rebukes them in his anger and terrifies them in his wrath, saying, "I have installed my King on Zion, my holy hill." I will proclaim the decree of the Lord: He said to me; "You are my Son; today I have become your Father."[1]

110

The section begins by reminding us that when we say that at the centre of the universe there is a throne, we are not speaking in physical or geographical terms. God is infinite:

> Where can I go from your Spirit?
> Where can I flee from your presence?
> If I go up to the heavens, you are there;
> if I make my bed in the depths, you are there.
> If I rise on the wings of the dawn,
> if I settle on the far side of the sea,
> even there your hand will guide me,
> your right hand will hold me fast.[2]

God is without bounds or limits. As Solomon said when he was dedicating the temple in Jerusalem: "The heavens, even the highest heaven, cannot contain you. How much less this temple I have built!"[3]

God has another temple – he dwells in the hearts of the humble and says to those who mourn for their sins: "I live in a high and holy place, but also with him who is contrite and lowly in spirit."[4]

However, when the throne of God is specifically mentioned, it has important significance. It is speaking about God in his kingly authority,[5] and his right to rule the nations as king of the earth;[6] it emphasises his activity as the righteous judge of us all.[7]

So this psalm brings us pictures of who God is and some of the different activities in which he is involved, but for the psalmist then to say that coming from the throne is the sound of laughing[8] is disturbing. The words of Handel's *Messiah* ring uncomfortably in our ears: "The Lord shall have them in derision." The psalm goes even further when it says that

God "rebukes them in his anger and terrifies them in his wrath".

At first glance these verses echo G. K. Chesterton's famous line from his epic "Ballad of the White Horse", where the Virgin Mary says to King Alfred, in response to his question as to whether he would win an upcoming battle: "I tell you naught for your comfort." So what are we to make of them?

Obviously, the mocking here is in the context of our rebellion, the unwise enterprise undertaken by those who have conspired against God's throne and all it stands for – those who imagine that their rebellion might succeed. Will the kings and rulers of this world usurp his throne? Will humankind do away with God? The thought is absurd – only worthy of contempt and derision, implies the psalmist. Yet it leaves us asking: How does the Bible's teaching on God's love relate to all this?

God is in no way callous or cruel – he loved us enough to die for us while we were still his enemies.[9] He loved us so much that he sent his only Son into the world that we might have eternal life through faith in him.[10] So his laughter cannot be the laughter of indifference. The One he sent to this rebellious planet, to save it from the consequences of its rebellion, wept over Jerusalem's refusal to save herself from suffering and destruction.[11] Therefore we know his heart is not hardened by all the rejection he has experienced. The laughter is rather from a sense of incredulity for all those who, in their arrogance, think they could ever run their lives, and this world, without him. It is the futility of their conspiracy that he mocks. Even to think their rebellion could succeed is ludicrous.

It was in the face of this rebellion that God showed his love. He sent his Son into the world. In our psalm God says: "I have installed my King on Zion, my holy hill," to which the Son replies, "I will proclaim the decree of the Lord: He said to me, 'You are my Son, today I have become your Father.'" And so the God above "became flesh and made his dwelling among us . . . the One and Only, who came from the Father, full of grace and truth."[12] He is "Immanuel – God with us."[13]

It was then that the earthquake struck as the rebellion gathered momentum: "He was in the world, and though the world was made through him, the world did not recognise him. He came to that which was his own, but his own did not receive him."[14] The world took its "stand . . . against the Lord and against his Anointed One".[15]

That was precisely what happened when Pilate presented Jesus to the mobs in Jerusalem. They screamed: "Take him away! Take him away! Crucify him!"

"Shall I crucify your king?" Pilate asked.

"We have no king but Caesar,"[16] they responded.

The crucifixion appeared to spell defeat. The powers of evil seemed to have triumphed. But at their rebellion, "The One enthroned in heaven laughs; the Lord scoffs at them."

The apostles witnessed his resurrection. The cross was not a disaster. In rejecting God's Son they saw that the authorities only ". . . did what [God's] power and will had decided beforehand should happen".[17]

That cross was in the plan of God before the creation of the world.[18] Jesus would rise again from the dead. The rebels were in for a shock. It is here at the cross that all history comes together, for it is both the clearest demonstration to us of God's love and at the same time the severest warning of his wrath, the wrath reflected in those words: "Then he rebukes them in his anger and terrifies them in his wrath."

Paul starts his exposition of the gospel of God's grace in Romans by saying that it begins with the revelation of God's wrath directed towards those who suppress the truth about him.[19] God's wrath is a manifestation of his holy, moral character, his repugnance at sin and evil – burning up and consuming all that corrupts and destroys in his world.

Paul then goes on to explain that this same gospel is the clearest proof we have of God's love. By love he does not mean sentimentality. We live in a world that has so abused the word "love" as to rob it of its true meaning. The love of God is pure and holy and not incompatible with anger. If God is not a God of wrath, his love is no more than frail, worthless sentimentality. That would mean mercy would be meaningless and the cross nothing but a cruel and unnecessary experience for his Son.

Obviously, there was nothing weak or sentimental about the cross. It stands at the heart of history and is the meeting point of God's wrath and mercy. Everything before the cross points towards it. Everything since the cross looks back to it. It is God's answer to the heart of the world's problem.

Here we face deep mystery – titanic forces in an unbearable tension. The omnipotent, righteous, all-loving Creator is rejected by the very people he created. How can he not punish them? We are told that he is a consuming fire.[20] The intensity of that holy fire is so powerful that, were he not almighty God, he would self-destruct. On the cross it almost seems as if that is what could be happening as Jesus cries out: "My God, my God, why have you forsaken me?"

James Philip, in the Bible study notes he wrote for his congregation, helps us to a deeper understanding of these words: "My God, my God why have you forsaken me?" He points out that they take us into the Holy of Holies. It is as if the curtain has been drawn back a fraction and we are allowed a glimpse of the intimate relationship that exists within the Godhead. What we hear the Son saying to his Father is stark and alarming. It hints at something unthinkable: disruption in the Godhead. Yet in that mysterious and awful cry from the darkness which hung over the cross we glimpse the deeps of God's holy love for this guilty world.

We tread humbly on holy ground. How could the Lord forsake his Anointed One? How could Christ not understand what was happening if it was all a part of the divine plan from before time began?

Only a few years earlier, at his baptism, the door of heaven had opened and Jesus had heard the voice from heaven say: "This is my Son, whom I love."[21] This would have reminded him of the second psalm and the fact that he was God's Anointed One. But now, after he had just prayed so fervently: "Father, the time has come. Glorify your Son, that your Son may glorify you",[22] there was little evidence of glory in the agony of all he was passing through. There was only abandonment, and little prospect, from a human perspective, of fulfilling the messianic hope the psalm had promised.

Crucifixion ranks with the most sadistic, barbaric and savage deaths ever devised by humankind. Through the centuries, artists have magnified its horror. But art can never portray the real horror of what was happening when Jesus hung on the cross. It may even be guilty of doing the opposite. Art, by getting us to focus our attention on the physical and external, may cause us to overlook the truly awesome nature of that event.

This was no mere martyrdom. Many martyrs have faced death courageously. If Jesus' death was only a martyr's death, then it would have been tragic but not remarkable. What Jesus faced was something far more terrible than martyrdom. He faced what no one has yet faced – "the second death",[23] that death which is the "wages of sin".[24] That is what the writer to the Hebrews means when he says that Jesus by the grace of God "suffered death, so that . . . he might taste death for everyone".[25] That is why his total identification with our humanity was so important: "Since the children have flesh and blood, he too shared in their humanity so that by his death he might destroy him who holds the power of death – that is, the devil – and free those who all their lives were held in slavery by their fear of death."[26] For him to identify with us completely he had to identify with the punishment we deserve.

The Apostles' Creed captures the unthinkable when it says: "He descended into hell." Hell is not to be thought of here in terms of physical geography but in its essence, abandonment by God – that abyss which is the consequence of sin – "the second death".

Yet the more we think about it, the deeper the mystery becomes. How could the sinless Son of God, one with the Father and the Holy Spirit from all eternity, be separated from the Father? How could he not know why?

In his great passage on the reconciling love of God in Christ, Paul writes, "God made him who had no sin to be sin for us, so that in him we might become the righteousness of God."[27] The six words "He was made sin for us" take us to the heart of Jesus' suffering on the cross. Sin cuts us off from God. The sinless Son of God was made sin. He stood before God as the most wicked of all people.

He was taking on himself all that our rebellion meant, and facing the consequences. God was exposing him to the wrath and anger that our sin merits. For Jesus to "be the firstborn among many brothers"[28] and bring "many sons to glory",[29] that was what was involved: he was *made to be* our sin. He became all that we are, all that is rotten, and all that is shameful in us.

Is it any wonder that Isaiah, speaking of the suffering servant, said that those who looked at him were "appalled . . . his appearance was so disfigured beyond that of any man and his form marred beyond human likeness".[30]

The One who was from eternity "the radiance of God's glory and the exact representation of his being"[31] on the cross was made sin and became so disfigured and marred that he was no longer recognisable as truly human. As Alex Motyer has said in his commentary on this verse, such was the revulsion that they who saw him "stepped back in horror, not only saying, 'Is this the Servant?' but 'Is this human?'"

It is on the cross that I see the horror of my sin. It is hard to express this, but that disfigured object of horror which Jesus became on the cross was a reflection of me and all the gross distortion of my sin. All the horror of what I am in my rebellion was exposed to the wrath of God in his Son. Christ suffers the judgement that is properly mine. The wrath which is revealed "against all the godlessness and wickedness of men who suppress the truth by their wickedness",[32] is at the same time the clearest expression of his holy love by which we are reconciled to him. As someone has said, "On the cross God saw me at my worst, and on the cross God loved me most."

And yet Jesus cries out, "Why?" The question is, why did he ask why? He had gone to the cross willingly. He had said that he laid down his life for the sheep; no one took it from him but he laid it down willingly.[33] He knew from the beginning of his mission that to be made sin would involve being abandoned. That was what had appalled him when he agonised in the garden of Gethsemane and said: "If it is possible, may this cup be taken from me. Yet not as I will, but as you will."[34] He had known what was coming. Yet from all eternity he had never experienced such a thing. And the horror as he experienced it was the ultimate horror. He descended into hell.

What was it that made him ask this? The mystery goes deeper. While he had known that being made sin would involve being cut off from the Father, in some sense that we will never be able to understand, he was cut off at that point of time from understanding fully what he was going through. As he hung on the cross and as, for three long hours, darkness came over the scene, he was not only separated from his Father, but even separated from understanding fully what he was going through.

If Jesus had gone through it all, conscious that everything would turn out all right in the end, his identification with us would have been compromised. Instead, he plumbed the depths of the horror of sin.

As James Philip wrote in his church's study notes:

It was *there*, at *that* point, where the Son of God lost the last, final consciousness of the Father's love – *there*, that atonement was made and pardon bought and won for us.

Anne Cousins' expression of these deep truths in her hymn can hardly be bettered:

> Jehovah lifted up his rod,
> O Christ, it fell on thee!
> Thou wast sore stricken of thy God;
> There's not one stroke for me.
> Thy tears, thy blood, beneath it flowed;
> Thy bruising healeth me.
>
> Death and the curse were in our cup –
> O Christ, 'twas full for thee;
> But thou hast drained the last dark drop –
> 'Tis empty now for me.
> That bitter cup – love drank it up;
> Now blessing's draught for me.

What, then, will Jehovah, the Lord of heaven and earth, do with those who despise his grace, spurn his mercy, and reject the atonement his Son made for us on the cross? And what is going to happen to all those who, in ignoring his authority, persist in their silent conspiracy?

The apostle John gives us an indication of the answer to that question when he writes: "Whoever believes in the Son has eternal life, but whoever rejects the Son will not see life, for God's wrath remains on him."[35] And the cross shows us just what God's wrath can do. For in judging sin, he did not spare even his own Son.

The cross stands in the world of time, at the heart of history, and it shows us that if God did not exercise his wrath against sin, his love would be no more than frail, worthless sentimentality, and the whole concept of his mercy would have no meaning.

So in the light of the cross, Scripture asks: "How shall we escape if we ignore such a great salvation?"[36] The simple answer is: there is no escape! The only hope for our world lies in embracing this salvation.

The world's rebellion is doomed to fail. There is no way it can succeed. We face a missionary confrontation with those who are in rebellion. Only through repentance and faith in him will they discover the salvation that will bring them to the liberty of "the obedience that comes from faith".[37]

As the missiologist Herbert J. Kane has written: "His wrath against sin makes salvation necessary. His love for the Sinner makes salvation possible."

The words of Graham Kendrick's beautiful hymn seem the only appropriate response we can make:

> We worship at your feet,
> Where wrath and mercy meet,
> And a guilty world is washed by love's pure stream.
> For us he was made sin,
> Oh, help me take it in.
> Deep wounds of love cry out, "Father, forgive."
> I worship, I worship the Lamb who was slain.

Graham Kendrick © Make Way Music.
Used by permission.

Notes

1 Psalm 2:4–7
2 Psalm 139:7–10
3 1 Kings 8:27
4 Isaiah 57:15
5 Psalm 11:4; 45:6
6 Psalm 47:7–9

7 Psalm 9:4, 7–8 cf. Revelation 20:11
8 Psalm 2:4–5
9 Romans 5:10
10 John 3:16
11 Luke 19:41–44
12 John 1:14
13 Matthew 1:23
14 John 1:10–11
15 Psalm 2:2
16 John 19:14–15
17 Acts 4:28
18 Revelation 13:8
19 Romans 1:16–18
20 Hebrews 12:29
21 Matthew 3:17
22 John 17:1
23 Revelation 2:11; 20:6, 14; 21:8
24 Romans 6:23
25 Hebrews 2:9
26 Hebrews 2:14–15
27 2 Corinthians 5:21
28 Romans 8:29
29 Hebrews 2:10
30 Isaiah 52:14
31 Hebrews 1:3
32 Romans 1:16–18
33 John 10:17–18
34 Matthew 26:39
35 John 3:36
36 Hebrews 2:3
37 Romans 1:5

CHAPTER ELEVEN

THE DEATH OF DEATH

. . . all flesh shall see his glory. (William Fullerton)

There was a very definite "kerrlunk" (something my spell checker does not recognise) but the sound of terminal finality from the front axle was more than recognisable. After sitting three to a hard seat and sharing the jarring ride over the potholed road with goats, hens and a prize fighting cockerel, it was almost a relief, initially, to be ordered out to the freedom of the roadside. The sense of liberty did not last, however. The driver and his assistant disappeared beneath the front end of the bus and after a few feeble tapping noises, appeared to relax quietly in the shade and fall asleep. There was certainly little evidence of any more progress on the engineering front. For the rest of us it was Ramadan, midday, and blazing hot. The trees being conspicuous by their absence, it all added up to no shade, no drinks, no food, and no transport. I could feel the heat burning through my shirt and reflecting upwards from the yellow dusty earth. Even my trusty black Clarks' shoes had turned pale yellow.

We waited and sweated. We had come from Makassar and were not far from the Buginese town of Pare-Pare, halfway to the Toraja Highlands. It was the point at which the metalled road ended. When another vehicle, optimistically calling itself a bus, finally hove into sight and offered to transport us to Pare-Pare, we all got in, or on, depending on our agility. I think those on top of the luggage on top of the bus probably had the pleasantest ride, but we were grateful to be moving again and I ended up spending the night in the home of a good Muslim family in Pare-Pare.

At around three o'clock in the morning I was kindly wakened by my host and invited to share in the incredible feast prepared to set up the faithful for the day of fasting ahead. The women of the household had been up all night cooking and I had hardly slept for all the noise and chatter. There in the room was an immense smorgasbord. As the honoured, if unexpected, guest, I was given the seat of honour and plied with plate after plate of delicacies. I remember a Muslim friend of ours complaining one year that she did not have enough money to fast. If this is what the fasting ritual involved, it was hardly surprising. Just as so many of us overspend on Christmas food and feasting, so it appeared this family made sure that their fast was preceded by a feast. You needed a few hours' respite before you felt like eating again.

I was heading north to visit some of our missionaries working in Toraja. Many Indonesians living in the green valleys of Toraja had become Christians. Some cynics suggested they had turned to Christianity to ward off pressure from Islam, as the latter religion would ban them from eating pork and drinking their *tuak* – fermented palm wine. Clearly, many of them had little grasp of what it meant to follow Christ. There was a never-ending tug of war with indigenous animist beliefs. The root issue was: Who is Lord? Christ or the ancestors? It is a society trapped in a social web of death. Death is the cornerstone of their culture. And these death rituals are the number one tourist attraction of the region, the income supplementing the people's lifestyle and easing the burden of their funerals.

The onward journey over unmade roads from Pare-Pare to Makale seemed to take forever. After another breakdown, fixed this time with lashings of rattan and bamboo, and after several weary miles of dry tracks winding round the hillsides, we found ourselves entering a beautiful new world. Craggy mountains, palm trees, bamboo and lush banana trees surrounded villages of traditional Torajanese houses set in an emerald sea of paddy fields. And, blessed relief, it was several degrees cooler. We stood at the entrance to a large secluded valley surrounded by hills and mountains, a landscape of limestone formations, terraced valleys and wooded hills with something of the Shangri-La about it. But like Shangri-La, not everything is as it seems. This is the land where the dead rule the living, and the living find themselves overwhelmed by the demands made on them by the dead.

Sunday found me preaching at one of the local churches. After the service an elder came into the vestry and wept. I had been speaking of Jesus as the bread of life but, as for so many others in Toraja, it was death, not life, that was this man's problem.

It is said of the Torajanese that they live to die. In Britain, funerals generally take place within a few days of death. In Torajanese terms, it takes a long time to "die". Death has become a mix of rituals, custom, social life and spectacle. The dead are regarded as being as much a part of society as the living. So across the rice fields where the people work, you can see cliffs rising precipitously with balconies carved high into the solid rock. These balconies are crypts. They house the mortal remains of Toraja nobility. And standing propped up in the balconies is a row of macabre wooden dolls representing the deceased. The effigies are dressed in sarongs and their sightless eyes look out impassively over the rice fields where the dead had once worked. Once a year their effigies are taken down, washed, re-clothed and replaced in their balconies.

Lower down the cliffs, a network of coffin-filled caves reaches deep into the limestone caves. As you walk inside, you are greeted by skeletons tumbling out of wooden coffins. Skulls sit side by side on rock ledges. Bones and old coffins lie open in gruesome disarray. Since the souls of the ancestors are residing in a spirit world elsewhere, busily ensuring the fertility of the rice fields, it is seemingly appropriate that their earthly remains should be on display for us. Little food offerings lie here and there just in case any of them need to "eat". The birds look fat.

The reason for it all is that the spirits of the ancestors have to be kept happy. After all, they are thought to wield a vast amount of power over daily life. They are seen as the lords of the earth. It is they who confer good crops, health, and fertility on their descendants. So if you dishonour or displease an ancestor at their funeral ceremony you could be in serious trouble. Crops could fail; wives and daughters could be subject to miscarriages. Accidents could happen. Others could die.

This brings us back to our elder in the vestry. He had experienced two tragic deaths in his family. These relatives had been given a Christian funeral. He had refused to go through with the customary death rituals. Then one of his own children had died, and suddenly he came under immense pressure from his family. They accused him of actually causing the child's death by refusing to perform the correct rites for the other members of the family. He was a man at his wits' end. So he had given in, and gone through with the ceremonies, but then had come to realise that what he had done was a denial of his faith. He was desperate. He needed to confess his lack of faith and find the Lord's forgiveness.

It is hard for us to realise what such a culture of death is like. It is woven into the warp and woof of this society. Distant family members will come back home from all over the islands of Indonesia for a funeral. Matters of inheritance are somehow determined by how much each of the children con-tributes to the ceremony. The "accounting" procedures as to who gets what, by way of what, are known as "meat debts": these are incredibly complex and worked out according to rules handed down through the centuries. Some of the village elders have memorised who owes what and to whom. The social order is built on this web of death, and surviving family members vie for position and influence as they try to outdo one another. The rich flaunt their status. The poor feel despair. And for Christians, breaking the cycle of such a culture can make them into social outcasts.

When someone is "ready" to have a funeral, whole villages from the surrounding valleys will arrive in a procession at the home of the deceased. Temporary houses will be built for the guests. They will stay for around a week or so, all at the expense of the grieving family. The family therefore can become burdened with debts that take many years to pay off. Feasts, chants, rituals, cock fights and buffalo fights all have to be laid on for the guests.

Central to it all is the killing of buffalo. Buffalo are a symbol of wealth, and in order for the deceased to reach heaven and be well supplied, they need buffalo sacrifices. The animals, especially the expensive white buffalo, are important and sacred. The status of a family and the success of the funeral is determined by the number of buffalo sacrificed. Around fifteen would be a normal number but sometimes as many as 100 may be killed if the deceased was rich or of noble birth.

Because the cost and planning are such a drain on resources, the event may not take place for months or even years after someone has died. There are two stages. Until the funeral, the body is treated with chemicals and kept in the family's house. During this period the dead relative is described as being "sick". After all, they are far safer kept in the house rather than being allowed to meddle around in the spirit world until they have been given a proper send-off; otherwise their spirits might just come back and blight your crops. To keep up the illusion and reassure the deceased that they are only "sick" until they have had their funeral, they are offered food each day.

As the journalist Jennifer Hile wrote in a *National Geographic* magazine article: "The smell of gradual decay is accepted as part of life in Toraja." The tragedy is that with all the turmoil of our world, the "smell of gradual decay" is part of life for all of us. The words of the old hymn spring to mind: "Death and decay in all around I see . . ."

But it is precisely here in the resurrection of the Lord's Anointed One that we discover the secret of God's victory over our rebellion. On the Day of Pentecost, Peter said: "God raised him [Jesus] from the dead, freeing him from the agony of death, because it was impossible for death to keep its hold on him."[1] He quoted from Psalm 16, ". . . nor will you let your

Holy One see decay",[2] indicating that David foresaw the resurrection of the Messiah and his victory over death and decay. The same theme recurs elsewhere in the New Testament where Paul reminds us that while death and decay is what we now see in the world, a day of glory is coming when "creation itself will be liberated from its bondage to decay . . ."[3]

In the heat of the tropics the decay and smell of death is inescapable. This is why, normally, funerals take place straightaway. The Torajanese are an exception. As if to counteract the smell of decay, mourners in some parts of Java will throw eau de cologne, flowers or spices into the open coffin. But nothing can hide the grim reality, the horror, the finality of death. Here in the West with our air-conditioned mortuaries, death has been sanitised. We are not so conscious of the cruel reality of decay. We rarely talk about death. Yet it is the one fact of life none of us can ultimately ignore. And while we may push thoughts of death out of our minds, when someone we know dies or is killed, later the fear buried deep in our minds will surface. And who, if we are honest, is not fearful? Death is so final – or is it?

Jesus came to break us out of the web of fear which death can bring. It was said of him that he identified with us in becoming human so that "through death he might destroy him that had the power of death, that is, the devil; and deliver them who through fear of death were all their lifetime subject to bondage."[4] Yet as he was taken down from the cross, it looked as if death had won.

Those to whom he came were united in their hatred of God's Anointed One and said: "Here is the son; come, let us kill him . . . we will not have this man to reign over us." They crucified him. They rolled a stone over his grave and sealed it. And they congratulated themselves on the success of their rebellion. But "the One enthroned in heaven laughs; the Lord scoffs at them".

Those soldiers commissioned to guard Jesus' tomb had the most futile job imaginable. It was pointless. There was something ironic in their trying to lock the Creator of heaven and earth in a cave. No wonder the Lord has them in derision. "Vainly they seal the dead." He is the Lord of life – he is the Resurrection and the Life.

Once again, C. S. Lewis in *The Lion, the Witch and the Wardrobe* has given us a beautiful picture. The great lion Aslan has been slaughtered by the witch on the stone table. He had offered his life to save the traitor, Edmund, whom the witch had captured. As Aslan dies, it appears that the wicked witch has triumphed. An atmosphere of black despair is everywhere. Aslan's two companions, Susan and Lucy, are numb with grief. They wait and watch while the dead Aslan lies on the stone table. Then, feeling cold, they go for a short walk. Suddenly, as their backs are turned, they hear a deafening crack. The stone table has broken into two, and to their horror, Aslan has disappeared.

But their despair turns to joy when Aslan reappears. They can scarcely believe what they are seeing. As Lewis tells the story:

"What does this all mean?" asked Susan . . . "It means," said Aslan, "that though the Witch knew the deep magic, there is a magic deeper still which she did not know. Her knowledge goes back only to the dawn of time. But if she could have looked a little further back, into the stillness and the darkness before Time dawned, she would have read a different incantation. She would have known that when a willing victim, who had committed no

treachery was killed in a traitor's stead, the Table would crack and
Death itself would start working backwards. . . ."

Death working backwards – it could not hold him. It merely
proved to be the gateway to the proclamation of Christ's
kingdom and authority over the nations. For as Paul wrote in
Romans, Jesus "was declared with power to be the Son of
God, by his resurrection from the dead".[5]

So in the second psalm we have the Son saying:

I will proclaim the decree of the Lord: He said to me, "You are my
Son; today I have become your Father. Ask of me, and I will make
the nations your inheritance, the ends of the earth your possession. You will rule them with an iron sceptre; you will dash them
to pieces like pottery."[6]

The day of his resurrection becomes the day of his coronation. This is why, when Paul preached in the synagogue at
Pisidian Antioch, he could say:

"We tell you the good news: What God promised our fathers he
has fulfilled for us, their children, by raising up Jesus. As it is
written in the second Psalm: 'You are my Son; today I have
become your Father.' . . . God raised him from the dead, never to
decay."[7]

Jesus is now ascended to the right hand of God and sitting
on the throne "far above all rule and authority, power and
dominion, and every title that can be given, not only in the
present age but also in the one to come. And God placed all
things under his feet".[8] Jesus was no mere guru or prophet
or angel. He was God. He shares the throne of heaven with

his Father,[9] and all people everywhere will bow to him as Lord.

In the second psalm he lays claim to his authority over the nations by recounting the "decree of the Lord".[10] And it was in the full awareness of that decree that he made his "enthronement speech" before his disciples, telling them: "All authority in heaven and on earth has been given to me."[11]

By announcing to them that the nations were his inheritance and the ends of the earth his possession, he was affirming his right. The Lord from heaven is the King of kings and Lord of lords. And on that basis he issued the great commission:

> Therefore go and make disciples of all nations, baptising them in the name of the Father and of the Son and of the Holy Spirit, and teaching them to obey everything I have commanded you. And surely I am with you always, to the very end of the age.[12]

All Scripture points us forward to that day when echoes from the second psalm will ring round the courts of heaven:

> The kingdom of the world has become the kingdom of our Lord and of his Christ, and he will reign for ever and ever.[13]

On that day, Habakkuk's great vision will finally come true:

> . . . the earth will be filled with the knowledge of the glory of the Lord, as the waters cover the sea.[14]

It will also be the day when a new heaven and a new earth will appear. God will dwell with us and we will live with him. He will be our God and we will be his people and on that day, "He will wipe every tear from their eyes. There will be no more death or mourning or crying or pain, for the old order of things has passed away."[15]

Even death will die,[16] a truth beautifully expressed in John Donne's sonnet written in the seventeenth century:

> Death be not proud, though some have callèd thee
> Mighty and dreadful, for thou art not so:
> For those whom thou think'st thou dost overthrow,
> Die not, poor Death, nor yet canst thou kill me;
> From rest and sleep, which but thy pictures be,
> Much pleasure, then from thee, much more must flow,
> And soonest our best men with thee do go,
> Rest of their bones, and souls' delivery!
> Thou art slave to fate, chance, kings and desperate men,
> And dost with poison, war, and sickness dwell,
> And poppy or charms can make us sleep as well,
> And better than thy stroke; why swell'st thou then?
> One short sleep past, we wake eternally,
> And death shall be no more, Death thou shalt die!

Of course we cannot begin to imagine what heaven will really be like, but the Bible's language makes it clear that on that day we will at last discover true joy and satisfaction: "To him who is thirsty I will give to drink without cost from the spring of the water of life. He who overcomes will inherit all this, and I will be his God and he will be my son."[17] All heaven will rejoice and on that day a hallelujah chorus will sound such as no choir on earth could ever sing:

> "Hallelujah! For our Lord God Almighty reigns.
> Let us rejoice and be glad and give him glory!
> For the wedding of the Lamb has come,
> and his bride has made herself ready."[18]

So the future is bright. The future is glorious. The people of God will enter into the fullness of joy that God has prepared. "Blessed are those who are invited to the wedding supper of the Lamb!"[19] They will go on to live in the city of God where they will discover the light of the glory of God, and the "throne of God and of the Lamb will be in the city, and his servants will serve him. They will see his face, and his name will be on their foreheads."[20] Scripture runs out of words in its attempt to describe the glory of the victorious outcome: ". . . as it is written: 'No eye has seen, no ear has heard, no mind has conceived what God has prepared for those who love him.'"[21]

On that day, around the throne of God, there will be a great multitude from every nation, tribe, people and language, and the subject of their worship will be: "Salvation belongs to our God, who sits on the throne, and to the Lamb."[22] And on that day the Lord of the earth will, as it is so graphically translated in the *King James Version*, "see of the travail of his soul, and shall be satisfied".[23]

And how is all this going to happen? Our best answer comes through the words of William Fullerton's old hymn:

> I cannot tell how He will win the nations,
> How He will claim His earthly heritage,
> How satisfy the needs and aspirations
> Of East and West, of sinner and of sage.
> But this I know, all flesh shall see His glory,
> And He shall reap the harvest He has sown,
> And some glad day His sun shall shine in splendour
> When He the Saviour, Saviour of the world is known.

What greater contrast could there be to the hopeless bondage and helplessness of the Torajanese culture of death?

Notes

1 Acts 2:24
2 Acts 2:27
3 Romans 8:18–21
4 Hebrews 2:14–15 (*King James Version*)
5 Romans 1:4
6 Psalm 2:7–9
7 Acts 13:32–34
8 Ephesians 1:20–22
9 Psalm 11:4; 45:6; Revelation 3:21; Luke 1:32; Acts 2:30; cf. Acts 13:32–37; Hebrews 8:1; Psalm 9:4, 7–8; Revelation 20:11; Psalm 47:7–9
10 Psalm 2:7
11 Matthew 28:18
12 Matthew 28:19–20
13 Revelation 11:15
14 Habakkuk 2:14
15 Revelation 21:1–4
16 Revelation 20:14
17 Revelation 21:6–7
18 Revelation 19:6–7
19 Revelation 19:9
20 Revelation 22:3–4
21 1 Corinthians 2:9
22 Revelation 7:10
23 Isaiah 53:11 (*King James Version*)

CHAPTER TWELVE

THE KISS OF LIFE

Your kingdom come, your will be done on earth as it is in heaven.[1]

If Jesus is the Lord of all and if a day is coming when every knee will bow before him, and if he has commanded us to makes disciples of all nations, then the logic is not hard to follow. We face a missionary challenge to take the message of the uniqueness of Christ and his lordship to all men and women everywhere.

The second psalm reminds us that mission did not suddenly appear on the pages of the New Testament. It was in the heart of God from the dawn of time. The mandate for mission is found in the very first verse of Scripture. "In the beginning God . . ." – it is God's world. He made it. We are his creation. He has a sovereign right to our allegiance. And as God Almighty, he will have that obedience.

The message of the second psalm is simple. Either we bow in worship and accept his love and mercy, or we will be forced one day to face the terror of his wrath.

Our missionary appeal is summed up in the closing warning of the psalm.

> Therefore, you kings, be wise; be warned, you rulers of the earth. Serve the Lord with fear and rejoice with trembling. Kiss the Son, lest he be angry and you be destroyed in your way, for his wrath can flare up in a moment. Blessed are all who take refuge in him.[2]

One day everyone will bow to the Son of God. There will be no choice in the matter. He will judge the nations.[3] For all those who have accepted his mercy it will be joy. For those who have persisted in their rebellion, terror. That applies at a personal level but it has significance for the whole of society.

The Bible is full of exciting promises assuring us of God's love, his mercy, his saving grace and his faithfulness. And as believers we are encouraged to claim those promises and delight in them all. However, there are other promises, which warn of the consequences of persisting in rebellion. These are equally valid. They speak of God's wrath. They warn against making a shipwreck of our lives. These are truths that as disciples of Christ we dare not soft-pedal simply because our society, in the conspiracy of its rebellion, has decided to label them as "politically incorrect".

One statement from the writer to the Hebrews is a reminder that those who continue in rebellion will discover a side of God they would rather not know: "It is a dreadful thing to fall into the hands of the living God."[4] We are to alert men and women to that aspect of God's promises.

The last book of the Bible tells us that at the end of time a day is coming when heaven will cry out: "The kingdom of the world has become the kingdom of our Lord and of his Christ, and he will reign for ever and ever."[5] It goes on to give thanks to God that he has established his reign in power in the words of the second psalm: "The nations were angry; and your wrath has come. The time has come for judging the dead."[6]

The rage and rebellion against Christ is doomed from the start. It is futile. It cannot possibly succeed.[7] And at the end of time the awesome wrath of Almighty God will deal with the feeble fury of the kings and rulers of this world and all who have said, "Let us break their chains . . . and throw off their fetters."[8]

The book of Revelation then goes on to paint a graphic and frightening picture of God's wrath – a truly awesome picture of what that will mean for all who continue in their silent conspiracy:

> Then the kings of the earth, the princes, the generals, the rich, the mighty, and every slave and every free man hid in caves and among the rocks of the mountains. They called to the mountains and the rocks, "Fall on us and hide us from the face of him who sits on the throne and from the wrath of the Lamb! For the great day of their wrath has come, and who can stand?"[9]

It is not popular to speak of God getting angry. It is not comfortable and it is not an easy thing to do. But the psalm warns that "his wrath can flare up in a moment" and that is a message we must take seriously as we fulfil Jesus' great commission, not in any spirit of belligerence, but with that winsomeness and concern that reflects the love that God demonstrated at Calvary. His is a holy love so intolerant of sin that it has borne the full consequences of its own intolerance.

At the cross, God's wrath and mercy met. By the cross, two destinies become clear. One accepts his mercy. The other chooses to face his wrath. One will kiss the Son and will be able to say: "Since we have now been justified by his blood, how much more shall we be saved from God's wrath through him!"[10] The other on that final day will echo those awesome words, "My God, my God, why have you forsaken me?" – words which will be lost forever in that place of meaninglessness and abandonment which is hell.

The world may be hostile. But a realisation of the fate of those who persist in their rebellion adds urgency to our obedience to the great commission. "We are therefore Christ's ambassadors", and every one of us who submits to him as Lord is sent by him to implore men and women to be reconciled to God. It is in the awareness of having been commissioned with the message of reconciliation that we are to urge men and women "not to receive God's grace in vain".[11]

We are sent to be salt and light to a world in rebellion. We are sent to establish another kingdom – not a kingdom of this world, but a kingdom where Christ as Lord rules and directs the hearts of men and women who will bow to him.

And when we pray: "Your kingdom come, your will be done on earth as it is in heaven",[12] we pray a missionary prayer, and in so doing we put our own service and ministry on the line, to be at God's disposal. We cannot ignore what this prayer means in the context of what the second psalm is saying. The coming of his kingdom, while it is a blessing for his people, is anything but a blessing for those who have not kissed the Son and bowed to his authority. This warning must be taken seriously. It needs to be sounded above a diluted version of the gospel which places its emphasis on health, wealth and happiness. Why so? "For his wrath can flare up in a moment."

If we look at the very first psalm in the Psalter we will see that it speaks of two humanities existing side by side in our world, one evil and the other good, the one in rebellion, the other in submission. One says, "My will be done, my kingdom come." The other delights in God's word, praying, "Your kingdom come, your will be done on earth as it is in heaven."

The Bible speaks of two families. One it calls the family of Adam, the other the family of Christ. By birth we are sons and daughters of Adam. That is our natural family – in rebellion and oriented towards going its own way without reference to God. It is from that family that we inherit a nature that will lie and cheat, if we think we can get away with it. It is characterised by a personality that lives for itself, the side of us that responds instinctively to the messages fed to us by the media: "Go on, spoil yourself" or "If it feels good, do it."

This self-centred family of the "old Adam" is what we are born into, and it is committed to the silent conspiracy. Our mission, as followers of Christ, is to call men and women to join the family of the "new Adam" – Christ's family. His is a family we can only enter by being born again by the Spirit of God. It is a family of those who seek to live for God and his kingdom. "And he died for all, that those who live should no longer live for themselves but for him who died for them and was raised again."[13]

This is what the death of Christ for us was all about. It was a denial of all that being "in Adam" means. It was an embracing of all that being "in Christ" means, as God in Christ shares the life of his humanity with us. That is where we discover the radical answer to the world's rebellion. We are called to go into all the world and make disciples.

After the particular manifestation of evil at Dunblane, Eric Alexander wrote:

> Our . . . response must be to tremble at the frightening potential of evil in the world and (don't forget) in our own hearts too. We live in a society which takes evil lightly, regards it as a plaything, frowns on those who want to curb its freedom, and gorges itself (worse, allows its children to gorge themselves) on televised, videoed, filmed or live portrayals of the worst excesses of human depravity. Indeed, our society idolises those who represent that. And then we are surprised that we have produced the likes of Thomas Hamilton. What a callous insult to Dunblane's sorrows it would be, if our national boldness and carelessness about evil remained unaffected. . . .

He went on to say that we must show:

> . . . a new confidence in the gospel of Jesus Christ with its life-changing power, and a new desire to commend the only Saviour of sinners, in ever more winsome ways to a sick, violent and godless world. Nothing but the radical transforming power of Jesus Christ can bring hope to such a world.

This transforming power of Jesus, the gospel, is no mere smearing of ointment on the forehead but the destruction of the old in order to start the new. By his death and resurrection, that break with the old becomes possible. "If anyone is in Christ, he is a new creation; the old has gone, the new has come!"[14]

Hence we are to take the message that all men and women everywhere are to kiss the Son, lest he be angry. Subjects of the king showed homage and allegiance to their king by kissing his hand. To kiss here speaks of worship and submission.[15] So the call is for worship and submission to Christ's lordship and authority.

The appeal, while it applies to everyone, is clearly addressed very pointedly to leaders and governments. They bear a special responsibility in office for the example they set. As Calvin says in his *Institutes*, world leaders are not to "lay aside their authority and return to private life, but to make the power with which they are invested subject to Christ, that he may rule over all". Wise leaders will exercise their authority and leadership by leading lives of submission, not rebellion, to God and his revealed word. That is the only antidote to the arrogance of power evident in many leaders as they strut the world stage. The same principle applies to them in their leadership of the nations they represent, for "the fear of the Lord is the beginning of wisdom, and knowledge of the Holy One is understanding".[16]

Sadly, today when we hear God's name invoked, it is little more that the first utterance of some verbally challenged individual expressing surprise. Tragically, the sacred name has been reduced to the level of an exclamation mark. The fear of God has been lost, and with it the wisdom that comes from above. There is no lack of knowledge, but knowledge divorced from the fear of the Lord is a dangerous thing.

It is said that we get the leaders we deserve. When our leaders show a loss of respect for their Christian heritage, they are only reflecting the culture from which they have come. We should not be surprised if the breakdown of law and order in our society increases. By comprehensively ignoring God's word, we have lit the fuse for our nation's downfall. Our ultimate problem in the

Western world is not terrorism. Our ultimate problem is that we have failed to submit to the authority of God.

"Righteousness exalts a nation, but sin is a disgrace to any people."[17] History has many terrible stories to tell us on that theme. The out-and-out anti-God super-rogues stand as warning beacons: Genghis Khan, Herod, Hitler, Stalin, Pol Pot, Mao Tse Tung, Osama bin Laden, along with the Saddam Husseins of this world who are prepared to gas and slaughter their own people. Their arrogance and greed has brought untold suffering to millions. Any leader who fails to see how crucial it is to acknowledge the sovereignty of God and recognise the responsibility of stewardship they hold in their position of leadership, is open to the danger of pride.

As a child, whenever I heard the creed recited, I thought they were saying that Jesus "suffered under Pompous Pilate". When we read John's account of Jesus standing before the governor, we realise that "pompous" fits this man perfectly. Here is this puny man standing before the One who not only made him in the first place, but who had flung the stars into space. Here he stands, face to face with the One who is his Sovereign Lord (whether he likes the thought or not) and he has the temerity to say to him, "Don't you realise I have power either to free you or to crucify you?"

There is something ludicrous in the scenario. The One who made the heavens and the earth, who with but a thought could have blown this man away; the One who controls the destiny of planet earth; Immanuel, God-with-us, stands meekly before this pompous little man and lets him continue. What meekness there is in his quiet reply: "You would have no power over me if it were not given to you from above."[18] Did the earth tremble as he spoke, I wonder?

Pilate had got it wrong, as have so many of his modern successors. As the more humble of them will freely confess, politicians do not have the power they would like or imagine they have. Ultimately, God alone directs world history. He is the One to raise up and put down world powers, even though they may fail to realise what is going on behind the scenes.

To say that is not to impugn the commitment and goodwill of so many of our leaders. Many are good and sincere men and women of integrity. We know that by the common grace of God they are granted a measure of success, and we enjoy a measure of peace under their leadership. But if they fail to acknowledge their limitations and fail to recognise that there is a God in heaven, they court the danger that goes with an unwarranted sense of self-importance.

The prime example of that kind of pride going before a fall is in Daniel's story of Nebuchadnezzar. When that man, in the land today called Iraq, looked over his kingdom, he is reported as saying: "Is not this the great Babylon I have built as the royal residence, by my mighty power and for the glory of my majesty?"[19] God in his mercy didn't let him get away with his conceit. He was driven out to live in a field like an animal for seven years. He only returned to his throne in the palace when, duly humbled, he had finally learned the truth that "the Most High is sovereign over the kingdoms of men and gives them to anyone he wishes".[20] Our leaders would do well to think hard about that.

In the first sermon he preached after the Allied occupation of Stuttgart, Helmut Thielicke described the fall of Germany, as Hitler's Third Reich lay in the dust of its own death. Stuttgart was piled high with rubble from the Allied bombing raids, even as he preached. The decimation of Germany's

144 NOTHING ELSE TO FEAR

armies on the eastern front and the superior strength of her enemies were the external manifestations that finally brought the Nazi regime to its knees. Thielicke saw the deeper truth of what happens when a nation and its leaders have lost their fear of God. Despite their Christian heritage, the German people had become unaware of how they had been deceived.

Preaching to them on the Lord's Prayer – his sermon is recorded in the book *The Prayer that Spans the World* – he speaks of "the real and the most terrible danger: the danger that there is such a thing as the devil who can lead a man about by the nose in the midst of all his idealism, and – that there is a God, upon whom we can wreck ourselves, because he will not be mocked".

He spells out the miscalculations on which the German nation was ultimately "so hideously shipwrecked". It was not, he says, the strength of their enemies but the fact:

- that we did not calculate the factor which is "God" in our plans and therefore fell victims to megalomania;
- that we violated the commandments of God and therefore got tangled in the towrope of our own unpredictable and brutal instincts;
- that we ignored that monumental call: "I am the Lord your God, you should have no other Gods before me", and hence were landed in the giddy ecstasy of power worship which brought the whole world into the field against us;
- that we ceased to trust ourselves to the miracle of God's guidance and therefore put our faith in miracle weapons that never came;
- that we no longer knew that God is in heaven and man is on earth and therefore could not help but lose all sense of the real proportions of life and consequently were also stricken with

blindness in the purely external spheres of political and military relationships.

Behind the visible, "the invisible is mightier and more creative and destructive in history than the visible". Thielicke continues,

> Anybody who still has not grasped that our nation . . . *was wrecked precisely on this dangerous rock called "God" and nothing else* has no eyes to see. He no longer sees the forest for the trees, and because he sees only individual catastrophes he no longer sees the basic, cardinal catastrophe which is behind them all.

It is easy to agree that Hitler, Pol Pot and Mao Tse Tung all deserve to burn in hell. But the warning is for all of us: "There is a God, upon whom we can wreck ourselves, because he will not be mocked." Ultimately, for each of these men, it was God who was their downfall. They were wrecked on God. They stand before us as warnings.

It may not be in fashion to assume the dogma of racial superiority to which Hitler held. The West, however, could still be deceiving itself by trusting in an assumed moral superiority as it wages its War on Terror. Forget the One who has said, "I am the Lord your God; you shall have no other gods before me", and the real proportions of life may be lost.

Hegel, the German philosopher, is often quoted as saying: "History teaches us that history teaches us nothing!" What it ought to teach us is that our real enemy may not be who we think it is. The West stands in danger of being deceived by the arrogance of power, the same arrogance that destroyed the Nazi regime. Thielicke's warning comes from the bitter ashes of that misplaced trust: "We can never put too much trust in Jesus and we can never put too little trust in ourselves."

Notes

1 Matthew 6:10
2 Psalm 2:10–12
3 Matthew 25:31–32
4 Hebrews 10:31
5 Revelation 11:15
6 Revelation 11:18
7 Revelation 19:11–21
8 Psalm 2:3
9 Revelation 6:15–17
10 Romans 5:9
11 2 Corinthians 6:1
12 Matthew 6:10
13 2 Corinthians 5:15
14 2 Corinthians 5:17
15 cf. 1 Kings 19:18; Hosea 13:2
16 Proverbs 9:10
17 Proverbs 14:34
18 John 19:10–11
19 Daniel 4:30
20 Daniel 4:25

CHAPTER THIRTEEN

THE NEXT STEP

Blessed are all who take refuge in him.[1]

It was the rainy season. And it rained as only it can in the tropics. Somehow, rain is easier to cope with on holiday when you are on the shores of the Indian Ocean, enjoying vast stretches of tropical sand. You get wet from swimming; you get wet from the rain; the sun comes out and you get dry and it isn't cold. And if you do feel chilled there is all the vast open expanse of a deserted beach with the finest of golden sands on which to play ball, run and jump, and let off steam. And that is exactly what we did with our four boys.

One day, however, the rains were severe. The coast was being lashed by a cyclone. It was a real struggle to climb up the cliffs to shelter. Our eldest, John, put his small hand in mine and gripped tightly as we struggled against the rain stinging in our faces. For a second we paused for breath. John looked at me, and out came one of those profound theological insights which six-year-olds seem to produce from time to time: "It's all right for him up there, throwing it all down on us here!"

We know what he meant. Sometimes we feel angry. Often we experience fear of the unknown. We have a niggling apprehension that God is remote and unconcerned, a worry that he does not realise that we need his help and guidance, a fear that we might not survive forces over which we have no control. Like the psalmist, I look around and ask: "Why do the nations rage?" And if, like the psalmist, I realise it is because men and women have rebelled against God, I still ask: What does the future hold?

As to the shape of the future, none of us can claim to have a hotline to heaven. God has not given us a one-inch ordnance survey map. And we need to be careful of anyone who claims exclusive visions as to what may or may not come to pass. God's word does not encourage us to speculate. The emerging paths of history that God has mapped out are his business, not ours.[2] What he has told us in his word is meant for our obedience. We are not privy to the hidden secrets of his wisdom.[3] He knows it would not be good for us to know the future.[4]

That is not to say, however, that he has not given us guidelines as to how we are to face the future. We have a certain hope and expectation based on his word[5] and we need to be confident as we tell others of the assurance we have. And while no one but God knows the details of what will happen in the future, by grace we know the One who is the future. He is the God of history and Lord of the earth. To know him is our refuge in troubled times.

It was René Padilla who, as he launched out into full-time service, was told by a senior missionary: "God will not give you a map but he will give you his hand." There are echoes here of words quoted by King George VI as he gave his Christmas message in 1939 when Europe had just been plunged into the horrors of the Second World War:

> And I said to the man who stood at the gate of the year:
> Give me a light that I may go safely into the unknown.
> And he replied:
> Go out into the darkness
> And put your hand into the hand of God.
> That shall be to you better than light
> And safer than a known way.

The trouble is that we want to know exactly what lies ahead of us. We have problems wanting to know what we should do next. A young girl talking to me in my vestry one afternoon said: "If only God would say 'Mary, do this! Signed God', I would do it, whatever it was!" Many of us would sympathise.

We found some of her "sisters" in one of Tokyo's sophisticated shopping centres. It was a strange sight: a long queue of girls stretching along the pavement, away from the subway entrance – not going into the subway as we would have expected, but heading out of the subway onto the road. The line ran in front of a modern department store and ended at a little stall. One by one, they disappeared behind the stall to emerge unravelling a small piece of paper – the end of their lunchtime quest. It was a lucky note from the fortune-teller, guidance for the future.

In the ancient Akabusa shrine in Tokyo we watched a smart businessman in his mid-20s shaking a metal canister. Through a small hole a numbered stick fell to the floor. He took it over to a row of pigeonholes to find a small scroll of paper with his word of guidance for the day. What stocks should he buy? What shares should he sell? Whom should he marry? He was searching for light, desperate to know what the future held for him.

Modern, sophisticated Japan is in the forefront of modern technology. Yet its people are desperately empty and looking for guidance and answers from ways as ancient as time itself. From what we could see that day, Hosea had summed it all up perfectly when he said: "They consult a wooden idol and are answered by a stick of wood."[6]

The desire for a crystal ball is not confined to Asia. How many here in the West believe that the position of the sun, moon, and planets, set against the backdrop of stars at the moment they were born, somehow affects our personality, career, love-life and future? How many turn to astrology for light on life's major decisions? Newspapers carry columns simply because astrology sells newspapers. To say that it works is only to say that there are a lot of credulous yet satisfied customers. It can be deceptive and even sinister.

There is no such thing as a crystal ball. God has given us his word. In that word we will find light for our path. But that in no way means that we should abuse Scripture and treat it as if it were some kind of almanac on which to construct projections for the future. To trust to chance to find an isolated verse of Scripture for guidance is hardly different in principle from the businessman of Akabusa consulting his sticks.

God's word is to be understood God's way. Play the devil's game of Russian roulette with Scripture and you could be in for a shock. Isolate a text from its context and it becomes a pretext. It is as I seek to understand the whole counsel of God and behave as "a workman who does not need to be ashamed and who correctly handles the word of truth"[7] that I discover his word to be "a lamp to my feet and a light for my path".[8]

But has God not given us any intimation by which we can predict the future? Of course he has. We know that ultimately every knee will bow to him as Lord. We know that Jesus is Lord of the earth. We know he is coming back again. And while he did not spell out exactly what would occur in the final countdown, there is a sense in which he did tell us when that would be.

During the last few years of our ministry in Java, we lived in Jakarta. Security was an issue. So when we went on holiday we had to leave someone to look after our house. The man in question was called Wagiono. As he waved us off, he vowed solemnly that he would guard the property and we need have no worries.

Our destination was a small wooden house high in the mountains above the tea estates of West Java. However, the rains meant that the wooded hills were shrouded in a permanent mist, and although we were in the tropics, it felt cold. We were house-bound. With nothing more than a few indoor games and books, the children showed distinct signs of holiday fatigue. So we made the decision to cut our losses and go somewhere else.

That involved heading back to Jakarta. As we drew up to the house, there were signs of mad activity. Wagiono rushed out nervously. Our sudden arrival had not been factored into his plans. The house was a scene of chaos.

Thinking he had another ten days, Wagiono had invited his family and friends from the village to spend a few days with him sampling the delights of the city. Beds were unmade.

Extra beds were laid out on the stone floor. There were people in every room. We could hardly believe it. They had gone through all our cupboards and drawers and, as we were to discover later, had been quite generous in helping themselves to what they decided we no longer needed. The look on Wagiono's face had to be seen to be believed. His jaw dropped, and in that moment of truth he simply said: "We didn't expect you." It was a modern enactment of Jesus' parable – and with it the warning, "So you also must be ready, because the Son of Man will come at an hour when you do not expect him."[9]

Jesus did, then, say when he was coming back. It will be when we don't expect him! That should be warning enough. And there is one further warning – we are not to speculate any further than that. "No one knows about that day or hour, not even the angels in heaven, nor the Son, but only the Father."[10] We should live and behave as those who expect him to come at any minute. And as we look at events in the world around us we should be in a state of high alert.

Meanwhile, we are entrusted with the stewardship of the gospel. Jesus did not promise that things would get easier. Many false teachers promise prosperity and affluence for all those who follow Jesus. Jesus, however, painted a very different picture of what we might expect after his ascension. Life would become more difficult as his coming again drew nearer. He warned of false Christs. He warned of those who would deceive. He warned of civil and military unrest. He warned that "nation will rise against nation and kingdom against kingdom". He told us that we would be persecuted or even killed as his followers and that many would turn away from the faith and be deceived. "Because of the increase of wickedness," he said, "the love of most will grow cold, but he who stands firm to the end will be saved"[11] – not exactly a "prosperity gospel".

As to the future, God is not in the business of satisfying our curiosity. He wants our obedience. The only way to treat Scripture if we want to find light for our path is to do what it says. If we get that right, we can trust him to lead us to the place where he wants us to be. That is what it means to make him our refuge.

"Blessed are all who take refuge in him."[12] While judgement waits for those who continue in rebellion, happiness and joy are for those who "kiss the Son" and make him their refuge. That is the positive word we are to take to the nations – the news of salvation and the news that true happiness and security are to be found in Jesus alone. To that end he has commissioned us to call all people everywhere to the "obedience that comes from faith".[13]

The psalmist asked: "When the foundations are being destroyed, what can the righteous do?"[14] That was the question in Habakkuk's mind as his world seemed to be collapsing all around him. He faced the threat of war and longed to know what would happen next. God did not tell him. But as he faced each tomorrow, he did so with a new conviction: "The righteous will live by his faith."[15] Or, taking the reading in the *NIV* margin, "The righteous will live by his faithfulness."

"Faith", "faithfulness" – which? Both are correct. The word means both. As *Today's English Version* translates it: "Those who are evil will not survive, but those who are righteous will live because they are faithful to God."[16] Generally, the word is translated as "faithfulness" in the Old Testament. The twin aspects of trust and obedience always go together in Scripture.

"When the foundations are being destroyed, what can the righteous do?"[17] Answer: he can go on going on in faithful obedience, being obedient and holding to the faithfulness of God. That is what it means to take refuge in God. That is what it means to fear God. That is the secret, according to the closing verse of the second psalm: "Blessed are all who take refuge in him."[18]

What does the future hold? As a young missionary in my 20s, a verse from what has been called "a psalm for old age" gave me great assurance: "In you, O Lord, I have taken refuge; let me never be put to shame."[19] If he is truly my refuge, I will never be put to shame. That is the promise. As Matthew Henry comments on that verse: "God will never disappoint the hope that is of his own raising."

As a student, facing the uncertainties of the future, I heard a powerful message. It came from the lips of a dying man. He was old and very frail. In his time, Dr George Johnstone Jeffrey had been Moderator of the Church of Scotland. Now his voice was weak. When he had finished speaking he slumped exhausted into his chair. We sat in stunned silence, heads bowed.

As he spoke, the sense of God's being there in that lecture room was almost palpable. He read right through Psalm 139, that psalm which speaks of God surrounding us with his care – surely the ground for all that makes for a wholesome fear of the Lord.

> O Lord, you have searched me
> and you know me.
> You know when I sit and when I rise;
> you perceive my thoughts from afar.
> You discern my going out and my lying down;
> you are familiar with all my ways.[20]

His voice may have trembled but it was rich with feeling. This was, he said, his favourite psalm. The effort of reading had exhausted him. He had our sympathetic ear. But it was more than that. As he read, we had a sense that we were hearing that other still small voice.

He began his message: "Young people often have problems with guidance for the future." There was a long pause. "God will always give you enough light to take one more step." A long silence followed. It was eloquent. Words were superfluous. We searched our hearts. There we found unfinished business; weaknesses in our prayer life; disobedience in our walk with God; various areas where each of us knew we needed to "take one more step".

He waited for what seemed an age, aware no doubt of what was going through our minds. Then, with one final surge of effort, he raised his voice till the words rang in our ears: "Take that step!"

A week or so later, Johnstone Jeffrey died. The legacy of those few minutes lives on.

Notes

1 Psalm 2:12
2 Romans 11:33–34
3 Deuteronomy 29:29
4 Isaiah 55:9
5 1 Peter 3:15
6 Hosea 4:12
7 2 Timothy 2:15
8 Psalm 119:105
9 Matthew 24:42–44

10 Mark 13:32
11 Matthew 24:4–14
12 Psalm 2:12
13 Romans 1:5
14 Psalm 11:3
15 Habakkuk 2:4
16 Habakkuk 2:4 (*Today's English Version*)
17 Psalm 11:3
18 Psalm 2:12
19 Psalm 71:1
20 Psalm 139:1–3

ENGLISH-SPEAKING OMF CENTRES

AUSTRALIA: PO Box 849, Epping, NSW 2121
Tel (02) 9868 4777. Freecall (outside Sydney)1800 227 154
email: omf-Australia@omf.net *www.omf.org*

CANADA: 5155 Spectrum Way, Building 21, Mississauga,
ON L4W 5A1
Toll free 1-888-657-8010. Fax (905) 568-9974
email: omfcanada@omf.ca *www.omf.ca*

HONG KONG: PO Box 70505, Kowloon Central Post
Office, Hong Kong
email: hk@omf.net *www.omf.org*

MALAYSIA: 3A Jalan Nipah, off Jalan Ampang, 55000,
Kuala Lumpur
email: my@omf.net *www.omf.org*

NEW ZEALAND: PO Box 10-159, Auckland
Tel 09-630 5778 email: omfnz@compuserve.com
www.omf.org

PHILIPPINES: 900 Commonwealth Avenue, Diliman, 1101
  Quezon City
email: ph-hc@omf.net   *www.omf.org*

SINGAPORE: 2 Cluny Road, Singapore 259570
email: sno@omf.net   *www.omf.org*

SOUTHERN AFRICA: PO Box 3080, Pinegowrie, 2123
email: za@omf.net   *www.omf.org*

UK: Station Approach, Borough Green, Sevenoaks, Kent,
  TN15 8BG
email: omf@omf.org.uk   *www.omf.org.uk*

USA: 10 West Dry Creek Circle, Littleton, CO 80120-4413
Toll Free 1-800-422-5330   *www.us.omf.org*

OMF International Headquarters:
2 Cluny Road, Singapore 259570.